EFFE
PARE

MW01064473

STRATEGIES THAT WORK
AND MISTAKES TO AVOID

ROBERT O. OWOLABI

Bob & Bob Publishing, Gaithersburg, Maryland

EFFECTIVE PARENTING
STRATEGIES THAT WORK
AND MISTAKES TO AVOID
By Robert O. Owolabi

Published by:
Bob & Bob Publishing
Post Office Box 10246
Gaithersburg, MD 20898-0246 U.S.A.

Library of Congress Catalog Card Number 98-93440

ISBN Number 0-9666450-0-6

Cover Design by Anthony Hubert

Publisher's Cataloging-in-Publication
(Provided by Quality Books, Inc.)

Owolabi, Robert O.
    Effective parenting : strategies that work and mistakes to
avoid / Robert O. Owolabi. -- 1st ed.
    p. cm.
    Preassigned LCCN: 98-93440
    ISBN: 0-9666450-0-6

    1. Child rearing. 2. Parenting. 1. Title.

HQ769.O96 1999   649'.1
                          QBI98-1358

Printed In The United States of America
By The P.A. Hutchison Company, Mayfield, Pennsylvania

Preface

Parenting is life's hardest job. Parents are charged with the enormous responsibility of bringing up the next generation of human beings, so life on earth can continue. It is a responsibility that requires all that is good in a human being. That is, honesty, patience, tolerance, understanding, love, good sense of humor, thick-skin, selflessness, the list is endless!

It is only a parent who would rather go hungry than to let his or her children do so. The protective instinct in parents can go to incomprehensible extent, sometimes. There was a case reported in the United States of America, of a father who, at the sight of her daughter's hand in the jaws of a crocodile, jumped instantly on top of the crocodile, hitting the monstrous animal repeatedly on the back with a stick until the crocodile let go of his daughter's arm. Also, worldwide, there have been numerous cases of parents donating vital organs to their children at the risk of losing their own lives.

Despite all the sacrifices parents make to improve the lives of their children, only luck, or providence, or some invisible powers, make children turn out alright. Parents only try their best. As a matter of fact, regardless of how hard parents try, they end up being blamed for the misdeeds of their children whenever they occur.

Parents deserve more credit than they get from society. However, parenting is a thankless job! The rewards of parenthood are surely not of this earth but in the world beyond, for those who believe in the existence of such a place.

Parenting, is surely the world's hardest job. But someone's got to do it! This book adds another dimension to making this world's hardest job easier and more bearable for those special breed of human beings who summon enough courage to undertake the arduous task of parenting.

Robert O. Owolabi
May 1999

Dedication

This book is dedicated to the memory of my loving parents:

Israel A. Owolabi
and
Adelphine O. Owolabi

Their loving and *EFFECTIVE PARENTING* made me to become who I am today.

May Their Blessed Souls Rest In Perfect Peace. (Amen)

Contents

Introduction

This book sets out to establish guidelines for effective parenting. The guidelines are not based on any academic research or religious doctrine or dogma. They are based primarily on the experience of the author. After all, experience, the sages say, is the best teacher! Some lessons are also borrowed from tradition, reason and pure common sense. Some expert opinions (albeit esoteric), contemporary and pragmatic, were also drawn from. An attempt was made to cover examples of children of all age groups but the book is definitely not a 'be-all' or 'end-all' on parenting. Parenting, being a life-long endeavor, has so many facets to it that it poses a big challenge to cover all aspects of it in a book of this nature. However, there is definitely enough material for any parent, whether seasoned or just beginning, to draw from and use as appropriate. Some chapters even include 'rules' that could guide parents to make informed decisions, or act appropriately under various circumstances.

Parenting is a sacred duty ordained by God, Allah, Yahweh, the Cosmic, or the Universal Soul Essence, depending on the individual's belief system. Hence, no amount of education or reading can make one a perfect parent, unless one first strives to attain perfect communion with God Almighty, Allah, Yahweh, the Cosmic, the Universal Soul Essence, or the god of one's heart. In short, the sacredness of such a secular art, makes it incomplete if one attempts to undertake it purely through intellectual understanding without divine guidance or intervention. The interjection of 'divine guidance' here has nothing to do with religion. It is only an acknowledgment of the supernatural or superhuman elements of the art of parenting in the true sense of it! Translation: No parent can do it alone! It requires a combination of the parents' good and appropriate intentions, divine intervention and community cooperation, for a parent to undertake the unique art of effective parenting.

CHAPTER 1

Who Is A Parent?

The main character of this book is the parent. It is therefore appropriate and even important to provide a clear definition of who a parent is for the purpose of this book. The most obvious, popular and universally accepted definition is that referring to a man or woman who is biologically involved in the birth of a child. If this were true, then a surrogate mother would qualify as a parent, which she may not necessarily be, because through the arrangement of surrogating, she is only assisting the real parents of the child to conceive the child. So, this first obvious and popular definition is apparently flawed. A more general and broad definition that focuses on the role of an adult in the upbringing of a child seems more appropriate.

So, what is a universally acceptable definition? According to *The New Encyclopedia Britannica, Volume 9, 15th Edition,* a parent is "one who has begotten offspring, or who occupies the role of mother or father. In Western societies, parenthood, with its several obligations, rests strongly on biological relatedness. This is not the case in all societies: in some, a distinction is made between a biological parent and social parent, with the former producing the child and latter raising the child and acting as a mother or father in as affective or legal a sense as biological parents are expected to do in Western society. This distinction is particularly common in the case of fathers, and to accommodate it anthropologists have developed separate kinship terms: a 'genitor' is a biological father, and a 'pater' is a social one." The *Academic American Encyclopedia, Grolier Incorporated, Danbury, Connecticut, 1994*, defines a parent as "....the legally recognized father or mother of a person. In its narrowest sense and under the old common law, the term refers only to biological mothers and fathers. By statue in most American jurisdictions, however, people who adopt children are also considered to be parents."

One thing is clear from the above two definitions: a surrogate for the birth of a child may not be recognized as a parent! This inference appears logical because, while adoption is referred to in one of the definitions, the word 'surrogate' was not used in the two encyclopedic references. However, it is reasonable to infer that biological and/or social relationships of an adult with a child qualify that adult as a parent. So, adoptive parents are recognized as parents! Now that the identity of parents or what makes one a parent has been established, then what? In others words, what responsibilities come with being a parent? The answer is the subject of the next chapter.

In Nebraska, U.S.A., it is illegal for a mother to give her daughter a perm without a state license. It's the law!

CHAPTER 2

Basic Responsibilities
Of A Parent

A parent is responsible for the health, financial support, and education of his or her child, states the *Academic American Encyclopedia (Grolier Incorporated, Danbury, Connecticut, 1994.)* In Western societies, especially in the United States of America, the encyclopedia continues, parents are regarded, by law, as natural guardians of their offspring. In the absence of biological parents, other adults are appointed as legal guardians of children. In developing or so-called, third world countries, especially African, Asian and Middle-Eastern cultures, it is societal expectation that whoever bears a child - both father and mother, must be responsible for the well being of the child. In the event that the biological parents are unable to raise the child, the immediate relatives (grandparents, uncles, aunts, etc.) are expected to step in. When relatives are either unable, or unavailable, the community in which the child is domicile becomes automatically responsible. There may be state laws requiring this parental responsibility in western cultures, there is never a need for their application in developing countries because of the aforementioned societal expectations.

One common theme that is apparent in all cultures is that parents have the right of custody, as well as the right of 'first-refusal,' so to speak, of their children. The right of 'first-refusal' implies that parents are first given the opportunity to take custody of their children and other adults are allowed to step in only after the parents either decline, or are unable to do so. While the failure of parents to discharge their responsibilities to their children may be criminal offense in western cultures, it is abominable in developing countries in general, and in the Middle-East, Africa and Asia in particular. So, it is obvious that universally, parents are bound by local laws and customs to take proper care of any child they brought into being by natural or surrogate birth, or which they brought under their custody through legal or cultural adoption.

The earliest years of a child's life are about the most critical, for medical and emotional reasons. The infant mortality rate of any society is a direct result of how well babies are cared for in that society during their first few years of existence. With universal recognition of the scientific basis for this age-old knowledge, health experts world-wide are known to embrace the "zero-to-three" movement, which focuses on children from birth to the start of school. For health experts in the third world, it is a major rallying cry, probably because of the high infant mortality rate.

> *When you were born, you cried, and the world rejoiced. Live your live in such a manner that when you die, the world cries and you rejoice." - Old Indian saying*

The opinion of health experts in this regard is best assimilated, if viewed from the standpoint of building a house. It is a well-known fact that the foundation of a house is about the most important structure in the house. If the foundation is not solid enough, or if the house is not built on a solid ground, the house would definitely have problems standing upright in the future, if not even collapsing outrightly. It is on the same basis that the "zero-to-three" theory of the health experts is very crucial to the development of a child.

A child gains thinking, perception of meanings, and values entirely through imitation and training -- from parents and then from a wider society of peers and adults. Likewise, collective knowledge and consciousness of meanings and purposes are passed on from generation to generation. Individuality arises from each person's unique voyage of experience. Scientists have stated, for years, that the young brain is very malleable. The consensus in the scientific community is that intelligence, behavior and performance in school can be shaped by a wide variety of factors in the environment, from a mother's nutritional status during pregnancy, which affects the fetus, to a toddler's exposure to lead in substandard housing. A constellation of stresses, many of them linked to poverty, range from inadequate nutrition to physical abuse. These stresses may start right from the uterus. Statistics show that mothers receiving no prenatal care, for example, are more likely to abuse drugs, show signs of lead poisoning and have low-birth-weight babies -- all of which increase the risk of developmental problems in their children.

> *Life is the art of drawing sufficient conclusions from insufficient premises.*
> *- Samuel Butler*

For instance, according to experts, the basic skill of language is largely acquired from birth to age 10. The concept of mathematics and logic is acquired by age 4. Motor development is usually achieved by age 5, and emotional control and 'social attachment' - the ability to relate and bond to others - are acquired by age 2. It is therefore inconceivable the tragic result that may ensue in the life experience of a human being, if from childhood, such voyage of experience or learning, or basic moral upbringing never materialized because the child's parents were deficient in the discharge of their basic responsibilities.

The explanation given above may sound a bit esoteric, but to develop a basis for making suggestions as to how to appropriately bring up a child right from infancy, it is necessary to borrow from available literature, based on experimental studies and statistical data. The basic essence of all the above statements appears to be education and communication. Education on the part of the parent implies knowing the implications of their actions, thus avoiding those acts that may result in devastating impacts on their children down the road. In terms of communication, some experts even suggest that it is not a bad idea for a mother to start communicating to the child during pregnancy. There have been reports of women who play classical music to their babies during pregnancy. This may be a wave of the future because recent studies show that classical music tends to enhance the intellectual development of children. Some women are reported to read to theirs, while others just talk, in general, to their fetuses! The communication should be more vigorous, clear and constant right from infancy. Of course, the style of communication should vary with the child's age! This last point is addressed more

In Omaha, Nebraska, if a child burps during a church service, his or her parents may be arrested. It's the law!

fully later in this chapter.

For instance, it is a parent's responsibility to set limits for a child right from the time a child can comprehend simple instructions. Setting limits enhances a child's safety. It makes the child to always do the right thing, especially with regards to respecting the parents themselves, as well as respecting others. Regardless of their ages, children generally have a tendency to stretch the limits set by their parents. As they stretch, they constantly need the security of limits. It is the parent's responsibility to provide that 'safety net' within the limits to ensure their child's safety. In other words, set reasonable limits with some in-built flexibility and always be on the look-out for the child's safety. Setting reasonable limits does not mean being too permissive or too flexible. There has to be a maximum extent to which the limits could be stretched. In short, very responsible and effective parents would guide their children in firm and loving ways.

Whether dealing with a toddler or a teenager, it is a parent's responsibility to learn and understand the level of instruction or communication that is typical for the child's age and psyche. Many disciplinary problems occur because parents are either oblivious to, or tend to forget the level of behavioral expectation of a child in relation to the child's age. For instance, a child under four years old cannot be expected to sit still for hours, even if the child is watching a TV program expected to be of interest to the child's age level. A responsible parent should plan to let go of some misbehavior, as long as the misbehavior is not of any dire safety consequences to the child.

A responsible parent must be direct in telling his or her child exactly what is wanted of the child. As an example, a parent can say: "You can go to Debbie's house after school. If you want to change your plans and go somewhere else, call me first." A responsible parent must work with the other parent (the spouse) so that the child gets the same message from both parents. Children are very skillful in playing their parents against each other. If they don't like what they hear from one parent, they go to the other, hoping to get a contradictory message, which most of the time, would be exactly what they want to hear. A responsible parent must not make a promise that cannot be kept. A child should neither be bribed nor rewarded elaborately for being good. At the same time, a child must be given adequate attention and encouragement when not misbehaving. A little praise is in order when the child cooperates!

Respect is reciprocal, goes the old saying. Hence, to teach a child respect, a responsible parent must talk to the child respectfully. At the same time, showing respect to one's child does not equate to begging the child. Begging a child tends to give too much power to the child. It is, agreeably, a fine line that a responsible parent must learn not to cross!

Bottom-line, a responsible parent must follow the following ten cardinal rules:

1. Communicate to your child in a clear, concise and consistent manner, in direct proportion to the child's age, temperament and psyche.
2. Always be vigilant with a baby, thus being ready in an instant, to distract and redirect the baby when heading for trouble.
3. Avoid yelling and cursing at a baby or toddler who is playing with an item that is not to be played with or doing something anomalous.
4. Avoid inflexible demands or unrealistic and impractical consequences, such as "Get in the car right now or I leave you behind!"
5. Enlist the help of older children in rule-making if, and when appropriate.
6. Give choices, not rigid orders.

7.   Help children learn from their mistakes.
8.   Be open to change in dealing with adolescent children.
9.   Use 'tricks-of-suggestion' in dealing with adolescent children to find solution to conflicts or problems. 'Tricks-of-suggestion' means using matured ways to suggest solution ideas, without appearing to dictate them, thus making the suggestions easier for the adolescent to accept. In short, show understanding and find a common ground.
10. Listen with respect and empathy but be firm and resolute if convinced a teenager is heading towards dangerous grounds.

In concluding this chapter, two critical points that span the spectrum between toddlers and adolescents must be borne in mind. Most children under four years old may sometimes misbehave to express their frustration, partly because they have not developed enough communication skills to do so in a more civilized manner. Also, it is normal for adolescents to be non-conforming or defiant to authority because they are beginning the long journey to adulthood, which sometimes involves separating from the family and establishing independence.

> *In Boston, Massachusetts, it is illegal to take a bath unless ordered by a physician to do so. In 1659, the State of Massachusetts outlawed Christmas. It's the law!*

Parents' challenge and responsibility are to recognize a child's increasing maturity while continuing to set appropriate limits. A responsible parent must recognize the need for an adolescent child to work toward independence gradually and with appropriate guidance. It is incumbent on the parent to find the delicate balance between freedom and control.

> *Leadership is the art of getting someone else to do something that you want done because he or she wants to do it.*
>
> *- Dwight D. Eisenhower*

CHAPTER 3

Parental Authority

A ny adult who qualifies as a parent is automatically endowed with an undeniably profound authority over that child. In management, it is common knowledge that assigning responsibility to a person without the authority to implement it, is inefficient and will never yield the desired results or products. So it is with parenting. The previous chapter enumerated, in details, the various responsibilities of a parent. It is therefore equally important to lay out the authority at a parent's disposal to discharge these responsibilities expected of them, either by the laws of the lands of their domicile, or by societal expectations.

In the book, *Human Development by Diane E. Papalia and Sally Wendkos Olds*, authoritative parents are described as those who "try to direct their children's activities rationally, with attention to the issues rather than the children's fear of punishment or loss of love. They exert firm control when necessary, but they explain the reasoning behind their stands and encourage verbal give-and-take. While they have confidence in their ability to guide their children, they respect the children's interest, opinions, and unique personalities. They are loving, consistent, demanding, and respectful of their children's independent decisions, but they are firm in maintaining standards and willing to impose limited punishment. They combine control with encouragement. Their children apparently feel secure in knowing they are loved and also in knowing what is demanded of them. As preschoolers, these children are the most self-assertive, exploratory, and content."

In homes where the above description represents the *modus operandi* (mode of operation), the book opines that "children (*in such homes*) know when they are meeting expectations, learn how to judge those expectations, and are able to decide when it's worth risking parental displeasure or other unpleasant consequences in the pursuit of some goal. Children whose parents expect them to perform well, to fulfill commitments, and to participate actively in family duties as well as family fun learn how to formulate goals. They also experience the satisfaction that comes from meeting responsibilities and achieving success. The essential factor appears to be parent's reasonable expectations and realistic standards."

While I agree with most of the specifications stated above, because they represent closely my philosophy of parental authority, I disagree with some aspects. For instance, what does *"encourage give-and-take"* have to do with a parent exerting authority and control? Do military commanders encourage give-and-take? Of course not! That is why they are effective. Also, I disagree with the notion of *"limited punishment"* as a corrective measure. In my opinion, the responsibility of a parent is to set the rules and make them known to their children.

Once the rules are broken, the appropriate and commensurate punishment must be borne in full by the offending child. It is not only good in shaping the child's behavior along the right path, it also prepares the child for REAL life. That is, if you do the CRIME, you must also do the TIME in FULL, NOT PARTIALLY. Actually, in fairness to Ms. Papalia and Ms. Olds, authors of *Human Development*, these were not their ideas. They were only presenting one of the three categories of parenting styles as presented by the findings of Diana Baumrind, a psychologist at the University of California at Berkeley, in her bid to "discover relationships between different styles of child rearing and the social competence of children."

Ms. Baumrind's three categories of parenting styles are *the authoritarian, the permissive, and the authoritative.* The *'authoritative'* parenting style was discussed previously. Ms. Baumrind described the *authoritarian* parents as those who "try to control their children's behavior and attitudes and make them conform to a set and usually absolute standard of conduct. They value unquestioning obedience and punish their children forcefully for acting contrary to parental standards. They're more detached, more controlling, and less warm than other parents; their children are more discontented, withdrawn, and distrustful." On the other hand, *permissive* parents, according to Ms. Baumrind's studies, "make few demands, allow their children to regulate their own activities as much as possible. They consider themselves resources, not standard-bearers or ideal models. They explain to their children the reasons underlying the few family rules that do exist, consult with them about policy decisions, and hardly ever punish. They're non-controlling, non-demanding and relatively warm, and their children as preschoolers are immature – the least self-controlled and the least exploratory." This outcome should not come as a surprise. That is what should be expected whenever a parent regards him or herself ONLY as a 'resource' and NOT a 'standard-bearer' or 'ideal model'. That is a position of 'do as I say, not as I do.' Enough said about that!

It would not be appropriate to dispute Ms. Baumrind's findings. After all, they were based on her studies with 95 families of 103 nursery school children. However, based on my experience as a parent, I believe that a combination of some elements of each of the three categories of parenting styles is the most effective approach to exerting good parental authority. In other words, in exerting authority effectively, a parent must be authoritarian, permissive and authoritative. A combination of the positive aspects of the three styles is all it takes. So, the following are my ten cardinal rules for good parental authority:

1. Exert firm control over your child's behavior and attitudes right from infancy.
2. Make your child conform to a set and absolute standard of conduct.
3. Demand unquestioning obedience from your child.
4. Punish your child to the full extent reasonably commensurate to the degree of rules violation.
5. Be a standard-bearer or ideal model to your child.
6. When your child is old enough to comprehend, explain to him or her the reasons underlying the family rules that do exist.
7. You, the parent, are solely responsible for making policy decisions.
8. Try to direct the activities of your child rationally, with attention to the issues.
9. Respect your child's interest and unique personality.
10. Be loving, consistent, demanding and firm in maintaining standards.

CHAPTER 4

Do Children Have Rights?

T he issue of whether children have rights, or not, has been well discussed over the years by both advocates of children's rights and traditionalists, who are more concerned about upholding moral values in children than advancing their rights. Proponents of children's rights can even be traced to the two most vocal groups involved in the abortion debate in the United States of America. Outside of the abortion debate, elements from both sides - that is, the "pro-life" and the "pro-choice" groups can be found aplenty in the children's rights movements. For the uninitiated, the "pro-choice" group is made up of those who favor the woman's right to choose abortion, if she so desires, as a means of terminating an unwanted pregnancy. The "pro-life" group believes that life starts at conception; therefore, every pregnancy should be carried to term, because aborting a pregnancy, they believe, amounts to murder of the unborn child.

The score on the issue of when life starts has not yet been settled and is beyond the scope of this book. Even, modern science has not been forthcoming on this issue because, frankly, nobody knows! But if natural laws are anything to go by, it appears a person becomes a living human being only when the soul enters the body. Metaphysicists believe that the soul enters the body at birth, which is when a baby draws the first breath independent of the mother. Hence, based on this premise alone, it is logical to conclude that a fetus may not be regarded as a human being until it draws its first breath. This syllogistic reasoning is known to mystics and others who are well versed in natural laws but since nobody has been bold enough to propound this theory, this author will not to be a pioneer in this matter either. Hence, it is prudent to say that the jury is still out on the issue of when life actually begins!

In terms of fundamental human rights, yes, children, like the rest of society, do have rights! However, being children, most of those rights (and rightly so) are curtailed (under normal circumstances) by the authority and supervisory prerogative of the adults under whose care the children are. As well expounded in chapters two and three, parents, being endowed with inalienable responsibilities and authority over their children, both through laws of the lands in which they reside, and societal expectations, must, and should worry first about the care and well-being of their children before caring about their rights. The author is, by no means, advocating total disregard for children's rights. The point being made is that when too much focus is placed on the "rights" of a child, discipline may fall by the wayside in the process. It is for the sake of "respecting the rights" of children that some parents become wimpish when it comes to disciplining their children. I am always amazed when I see some parents feeling helpless when their kids misbehave. I am talking of two to ten-year-olds! This helplessness is reflected in how they talk to the kids in such circumstances. They say things like, "John, please don't do that." Or, "Mary, please stop." Whereas, the right tone for children of such tender age should have been, "John, I say, stop doing that." Some experts would say that the "appealing" technique is more proper than the "commanding" tone because it accords respect to the child. I beg to differ! Children tend to behave like animals, sometimes. They do whatever they can get away with until somebody, or something stops them. If nobody ever stops them in any strong or commanding tone, or through some disciplinary measure, they would assume it is within their right to misbehave, and would grow up behaving in that manner for the rest of their lives.

Having said the above, it is also appropriate to acknowledge that a child has some inalienable rights which cannot, and should not be abridged. The following are some of those rights:

1.   The right to be comfortably housed.
2.   The right to be adequately fed.
3.   The right to be comfortably clothed.
4.   The right to be given good education.
5.   The right to be allowed to think freely.
6.   The right to pursue happiness, within parental limits.
7.   The right to make friends, with parental supervision.
8.   The right to ask questions for sake of quest for knowledge, not to challenge parental authority.
9.   The right to freely express opinion without hurting other people's feelings.
10.   The right to not be abused either physically or sexually.

However, in contemporary times, there has been a universal tendency to carry these so-called rights to extreme levels. The western world is more guilty of these than the rest of the universe. Children of the western world, in particular, are fast becoming undisciplined because of these so-called individual freedom and human rights. Unfortunately, this attitude is also fast catching on in other parts of the world as well. Almost every disciplinary measure is now regarded as some form of abuse. Many parents in the western world no longer feel comfortable to discipline their children, even in their own homes, for fear of being accused of child abuse! Some so-called "experts" have succeeded in branding every form of discipline as "improper." These experts advocate "appealing" to a child to do right, rather than "molding" the child to do what is right. Even the Bible states: "spare the rod and spoil the child." It was true in ancient times. It should also still be true today. In the United States of America, for example, the lack of home discipline in many children is also usually reflected in their behavior at school. Teachers are usually helpless when confronted by a brat. Any form of scolding by the teacher stands a potential rebuff by the parent, who, in the first place, created the brat by being deficient in his or her parental responsibilities. The school authorities are not helpful either in assisting or empowering the teachers to maintain discipline. It appears, in America, the children are in charge, both at home and at school! In urban areas, cases of teachers being beaten, or even killed by students are now becoming more rampant than before. It appears it is okay for adults' rights to be abridged, as long as children's so-called 'rights' are protected. Something is obviously wrong with that picture!

Hence, my ten cardinal rules for protecting children's rights, while preventing them from developing into swollen-headed brats, are:

1.   Children must be comfortably housed unconditionally.
2.   Children must be properly fed unconditionally.
3.   Children must be comfortably clothed at all times.
4.   Children must be appropriately educated.
5.   Children must be given ground rules of behavior at all times.
6.   Children must be given appropriate discipline for each violation of household rules.
7.   Children's rights must end whenever adults' rights are compromised.
8.   Children must be made to respect the laws of the land

in which they reside.

9. Children must be encouraged to think freely and ask questions, without questioning authority of their parents.

10. Children must not be abused physically, sexually, or psychologically.

In the State of Washington, U.S.A., it is illegal to pretend that one's parents are rich. It's the law!

A lie gets halfway around the world before the truth has a chance to get its pants on.
- Sir Winston Churchill (1874-1965)

A fanatic is one who can't change his mind and won't change the subject.
- Sir Winston Churchill

Mistakes are a fact of life. It is the response to error that counts.
- Nikki Giovanni

CHAPTER 5

Should Respect Be Reciprocal Between Parent And Child?

There is no direct answer to this question. The word "respect" can be defined in different ways and it appears to mean different things to different people. In a generic sense, the word 'respect' means "to feel or show honor or esteem for; hold in high regard," according to the *New World Dictionary of the American Language*, second college edition. The same dictionary also defines respect as "to show consideration for; avoid intruding upon or interfering with (*to respect others' privacy*)." The dictionary goes further in its definition of 'respect'. This is exactly the point intended when I said the word 'respect' can mean different things to different people. But the two examples cited above are most applicable to the theme of this chapter.

This author agrees with the idea that respect should be exchanged between parent and child. However, it is not clear whether the exchange of respect should be reciprocal between parent and child.

At the end of this chapter, it is hoped that readers would have enough information to make up their minds on this issue. The word 'reciprocal' is a mathematical jargon which ordinarily means something corresponding to the other; or, to quote the dictionary referenced above, it means something "present or existing on both sides; each to the other; mutual." The kind of respect exchange between a parent and a child is, sort of, similar to that expected between a superior and a subordinate. In short, since a parent has almost absolute power over a child, a child does not have much choice but to accord due respect to his or her parent. The Jewish Talmud states: "Let each man be in awe of his mother and father,....." The Islamic Koran states: "The Lord has decreed......to be good to parents, whether one or both of them.....; say not to them 'Fie' neither chide them, but speak unto them words respectful, and lower to them the wing of humbleness..."

On the other hand, the parent must exercise the 'milk of human kindness' in the adjudication of this, so called, 'supreme authority' by showing some consideration for the emotional well-being or self esteem of the child. In other words, while a child must show honor or esteem for his or her parent, the parent, in return, should show consideration for the child's mental well-being in the exercise of this 'God-given' authority over the child.

Let me say up front that children must first be taught how to respect other people, more importantly, their parents, and must have shown progress in this area before parents can even think of reciprocating the gesture.

> *Opinion is ultimately determined by the feelings, and not by the intellect.*
> *- Herbert Spencer*

The reason this point is being made up front is that on many occasions, I have seen parents acting very timidly, plain and simple, in their bid to show respect to their kids. The respectful gesture, constantly flowing one-way from parents to children, has led some children to believe that respect is always supposed to come to them without them ever needing to give respect to others. First, they start with their parents, and eventually, with everybody else outside the home. I have seen kids who would yell commands at their parents when they are requesting something. While, as an on-looker, I am boiling at such flagrant display of disrespect to the parents, these parents, probably out of not knowing better, would respond as if nothing was wrong with the child's attitude.

In my opinion, any child under thirteen years old does not need to be shown any respect by a parent, as long as the parent shows consideration for his or her feelings, when appropriate. Children under thirteen years old are still going through the process of deciphering things in general. They need to be told *what* to do, *when* to do them and *how* to do them. Teenagers, on the other hand, need to be told *what* to do and *when* to do them. The '*how*' part should only apply if they ask for guidance. Above adolescence, a child only needs to be told *what* to do. Under the above three scenarios, it is obvious that the interjection of respect must vary. It should be noted that this author recognizes that, barring any negative influences in a person's life, parents naturally show consideration when dealing with their children.

> *In the State of Arkansas, U.S.A., school teachers who bob their hair may forfeit their pay raises. In the same State, it is also illegal to kill any living creature. It's the law!*

So, to make a special effort to show respect would be an additional element in the parent-child interaction and should be applied with caution and at the appropriate age, so as not to make a child grow up with the wrong expectations from other people the child may have to deal with in adult life.

In discussing the subject of respect in parenting, it is difficult to avoid the subject of discipline. Discipline is the subject of the next chapter. But since the two subjects are so intertwined, the reader may take the cross-reference as a precursor to what to expect in the next chapter.

Even educators and psychologists, who traditionally admonish parents to go "soft" on kids, are now spreading a get-tough message that is resonating with many parents, says Jacqueline L. Salmon, a *Washington Post* staff writer in an article titled: *"Firm Support For Stricter Upbringing"* published in the November 24, 1996 edition of the newspaper. Ms. Salmon further stated that these experts contend that many baby boomer[1] parents are so concerned with building youngsters' self-esteem, protecting them from stress and making them partners in the family that they are raising a generation of selfish, ill-mannered, and troubled children. Need I say more! The *Washington Post* article also quoted Brown University education professor, William Damon, as saying the following in his book on the subject: "I have seen

---

[1]   *For the benefit of non-American readers, the term 'baby boomer' applies to those Americans who were born to veterans of World War II shortly after their return in the early 1940s. At the end of World War II, the United States of America experienced a sudden upsurge in rate of child-birth; most of the new babies were attributed to the recently returned war veterans.*

children upbraid their parents for not serving them well or quickly enough. I have observed children insulting, cursing, yelling at, or even threatening their parents. When I mention such incidents to colleagues, they do not strike anyone as remarkable or surprising."

Ms. Salmon offered the following solution, quoting from Professor Damon and others:

1.   Establish clear and consistent rules.
2.   Crack down strongly on misbehavior.
3.   Stop trying to get your child to agree with every decision you make (*see my cardinal rule number 7 in chapter 3: Parental Authority!*).
4.   A child of grade-school age sometimes should be sent to his room for the day.
5.   Parents should not rule out spanking. (*I say Amen to that! See my opinion in chapter 6: Discipline In The Home*)

The above may sound as disciplinary measures, but they also belong under the subject of respect in terms of teaching children to know how to be respectful to their parents and, eventually, to the society at large. It follows the simple logic that a well disciplined child would definitely understand what respect is and how to show it. If a child is brought up with only cuddling and pampering, it is my considered opinion that the child would grow up so rotten that he or she would become very belligerent when faced with an atmosphere devoid of cuddling and pampering. In such an atmosphere (that is, an atmosphere devoid of cuddling and pampering), which I submit, is real life, showing respect for others would be the last thing in the mind of such a child. So, should respect be reciprocal between a parent and a child?. The answer can only be in the affirmative when the child has been disciplined enough to know the proper way to show respect.

In Mesquite, Texas, it is illegal for children to have unusual haircuts. It's the law!

In the State of Pennsylvania, U.S.A., any motorist who sights a team of horses coming toward him must pull well off the road, cover his car with a blanket or canvas that blends with the countryside, and let the horses pass. If the horses appear skittish, the motorist must take his car apart, piece by piece, and hide it under the nearest bushes.

It's the law!

Silence is the best tactic for him who distrusts himself.   - La Rochefoucauld
Experience keeps a dear school, but fools will learn in no other.   - Benjamin Franklin

CHAPTER 6

Discipline In The Home

T he word discipline can be defined in many ways, depending on who the object of focus is, in the mind of the definer. At the national, state, local or community level, discipline is referred to in terms of citizens abiding by laws, regulations and ordinances well laid out in conventional legal terms. An average citizen does not need to go to law school to understand these laws. Most laws of the land are based on common sense. A law-abiding or disciplined citizen is expected to pay taxes, to not steal, to not disturb public peace, to obey traffic laws, etc, etc. In the workplace, a disciplined employee is one who follows the operating guidelines laid down by the employer. Even private organizations, be they professional, religious, social or recreational, have basic rules and regulations to which members are expected to abide in order to be in good standing as members.

An average household should also be viewed in the same light. Just like the entities mentioned above, households consists of members who must abide by some rules and codes of conduct to ensure a harmonious cohabiting of its inhabitants. However, unlike the entities mentioned above, where either appointed or elected leaders make the rules which are then enforced by law-enforcement officers, the parents make and enforce the rules in the home. It is an obligation the parents made when they elected to become parents! In discharging this obligation, every parent must remember the age-old adage that says, "when there is no law, there is no sin." In other words, if ground rules are not laid out clearly, there should be no expectation of behaviors in conformance with some imaginary or assumed rules. What is the point here? The point being made is that every parent must establish ground rules in the home. These rules must be made clear to the children. Additionally, the rules should be commensurate with the children's ages. The rules for crawling babies and toddlers should be different from those for young children. Different rules should be made separately for older children and adolescents. For effective parenting, ground rules should be made solely by the parents. There should be no negotiation with the children. Contrary to what some experts say, a home is an autocracy, not a democracy; especially during the formative years of a child -- that is, between the crawling stages until the mid-teens. Parents must always remember the age-old injunction: "Train a child in the way he should go, and when he is old, he will not turn from it." (*Proverbs 22: 6*)

Maintaining discipline in the home does not involve just making rules and expecting them to be obeyed. Any parent thinking that way needs to give up their children for adoption, go back and take basic parenting class, and then start the parenting endeavor all over! Of course, just like every other endeavor in life, rules would be broken! Kids are more clever than they get credit for. Children, being very good at studying their parents' emotional roller-coaster, play a lot of psychological games with their parents' state of mind; all with the motive of circumventing the house rules. If all else fails, children would turn to playing their parents against each other. These games work best where the parents are having a popularity contest with each other in order to be the favorite of their children.

There is no better and faster way for complete breakdown of law and order in a home than when *'popularity contest'* sets in. Granted, no two human beings are the same. Hence, two parents cannot be expected to apply the rules of the house the same way. However, for a child to be brought up with good discipline, parents must *brand* together and support each other all the time! One parent must not give consent to a request by a child until the other parent's opinion is verified.

Discipline in children appears to have deteriorated over the years. Indiscipline in today's children is so visible and commonplace that it has come into sharper focus in recent times, thus becoming more frequent in conversations among parents and other adults interested in the topic. There is even a general feeling that the pendulum, on the part of parents, is now swinging in the right direction, that is, in terms of steering children more towards being disciplined and morally upright.

In response to a question on whether parents are now swinging in the right direction regarding children discipline, John Rosemond of *Knight-Ridder Newspapers*, in a *Washington Post* article of August 20, 1997, opined that "a child who is at the center of attention in his family cannot be disciplined." He said that if by "in the right direction" one means that in the direction of parents expending greater effort to discipline children, his response would be 'no', because that is not the right direction. "Today's parents," he continued, "are rightly being told their children are, in general, an undisciplined lot. The brat, once a rarity, has become ubiquitous. Parents are being led to believe, however, that whatever discipline problems they have with their children can be solved if they use better disciplinary techniques more consistently. But practicing their disciplinary techniques, however consistently, is not the solution. The solution is for parents to take children out of the center of attention in families and assume that station themselves."

The facts of the matter, as identified by Mr. Rosemond are as follows:

1.   "A child who has been taught to pay attention to his parents can be disciplined relatively easily.
2.   A child who has not been taught to pay attention to his parents--who is at the center of attention in his family-- cannot be disciplined, but only temporarily put in check."

Mr. Rosemond's explanation is that a parent cannot teach a child who is not paying attention, and a child will not pay sufficient attention to a parent who acts as if it's his or her job to pay as much attention to-- and do as much for-- the child as possible. While he agrees that infants and toddlers must, of necessity, be the focus of their parent's attention, he also believes that it is in the child's interest that the table be turned around and things set right by the time the child is 3 years old. "Unfortunately," Mr. Rosemond continued, "today's parents believe (because 'experts' have told them) they are good parents to the degree they pay attention to and do things for their children. Because today's parents, in general, pay excessive attention to their children, their children do not pay sufficient attention to them. And so, children are unsurprisingly undisciplined, and their parents are unsurprisingly exasperated and ready to set things right. But the notion that firmness or consistency or timeouts or spankings will set things right will only set things more wrong. Again, a child who is at the center of attention in his family cannot be disciplined. To give parents more effective disciplinary tools, without telling them these tools cannot be effectively used as long as their families are child-centered, will inevitably frustrate parents. They will use the tools, but the tools won't work." Then "what will happen then?," asks Mr. Rosemond. In response to his own question, he stated:

♦   "Their frustration will drive them to use the tools more rigidly and more aggressively. Timeouts won't work, so they'll spank, occasionally at first; but an occasional spanking won't work either, so they'll spank harder; but harder spankings won't work, so they'll spank harder and more frequently.

♦   Other parents, pacifists by nature, will simply give up long before the first spanking is administered.

In either case," he continued, "children will remain undisciplined. In the first case, undisciplined children will have to endure unnecessarily harsh attempts at discipline and government social workers will have field days; in the second, undisciplined children will become ever more convinced that adults are wimps and undeserved of respect, and law-enforcement budgets will grow by leaps and bounds." Mr. Rosemond concluded his *social homily* as follows: "The solution to the problem of under-disciplined children is elementary: It is to make it perfectly clear to children once again that adults are the teachers and they are the students."

While I agree with all of the arguments advanced in Mr. Rosemond's article, I disagree with the pessimistic tone of his explanation.

> *Heaven often smites in mercy, even when the blow is severest. - Joanna Baillie*

His explanation seems appropriate for the situation of a child who has been pampered right from infancy, thus growing up an undisciplined and uncontrollable brat. However, since the question he was responding to was more generic about discipline, I found it difficult to accept his prescription. Even his suggestion that a 'child-centered' family would automatically have problems disciplining the children appears ludicrous to me. The opposite argument could be that if parents do not pay constant attention to their children, how will they be able to observe their actions and steer them in the right direction when appropriate? If Mr. Rosemond had substituted the word 'pampered' for 'child-centered', then his argument could have been more palatable and/or understandable, in my opinion. In other words, his statement would have been more agreeable to me if he had said: "A family with excessively pampered children would automatically have problems disciplining the children." The over-riding lesson of his article, which I totally agree with, is that once a child is brought up without adequate discipline, it may be counter-productive to, all-of-a-sudden, start applying strict disciplinary measures at each occurrence of indiscipline. In such situation, it is more prudent to start with the basics, which, as Mr. Rosemond suggested, include such rudimentary steps as making it "perfectly clear to children once again that adults are the teachers and they are the students."

The role of corporal punishment in disciplining children, while controversial, has its place and cannot be left unmentioned or unrecognized. The role has its roots in tradition and religion. It is an age-old universal phenomenon in the upbringing of children. Even the Bible states: "Spare the rod and spoil the child". Supporters of corporal punishment (popularly known as 'spanking' in the United States of America) say that when it is properly administered, it can be effective, if followed by an explanation of why the punishment was given.

Even pediatricians who support corporal punishment have said that it could be effective if used in moderation in the context of a nurturing relationship. It is simple common sense, they say. It teaches a child that some things are just not acceptable! But opponents of corporal punishment argue that it can only harm children and that other forms of discipline are more effective. Such stark opponents go further to state that there is no good way to draw the line between what is abuse and what is not, especially when there is a 'mark' or a 'bruise'. There is no research, they say, that has shown any beneficial effects of corporal punishment and there are too many disadvantages to it.

There is no distinct difference between corporal punishment and child abuse. State laws, in the United States of America, all say something to the effect that parents can use reasonable force but they do not say whether it is slapping on the wrist or slapping on the buttocks. In the enforcement of these same State laws, police officers in the United States often use the presence of a 'mark' or 'bruise' to gauge whether the punishment went too far. While even some proponents of corporal punishment admit that it can cross a line, they also believe that in many cases it can be just what a child needs to stay out of trouble. Popular media, especially the television media, have not been helpful in the balanced portrayal of corporal punishment. On television, a person who applies corporal punishment to an obvious brat is usually portrayed as raving. Proponents of spanking opine that it ought not to be that way. They say that spanking should come with lots of love. What it does, they say, is properly train a child, and there is a lot of respect that comes from that, they claim.

I know of nothing so pleasant to the mind than discovery of anything which is both new and valuable. - Unknown

But some recent research has found that spanking is likely to cause long-term behavioral problems, regardless of the amount of loving attention parents give to children. A study by researchers at the University of New Hampshire in the United States, published in August, 1997 in the medical journal *Archives of Pediatrics and Adolescent Medicine*, found that children who get spanked regularly are more likely over time to cheat or lie, to be disobedient at school, to bully others and to have less remorse for what they do wrong. Other experts on the subject of corporal punishment, who tend to be more sympathetic to spanking, said more research is needed before it can be said that spanking is always detrimental. On a lighter note, however, they claim that there is also no scientific evidence that spanking is either good or even necessary!

Now, here is my position on the issue. I am a firm believer in the use of spanking as a disciplinary measure. I used it in the upbringing of all of my four children and it helped shape their behavior as they grew up. But, just like anything else, it must be used moderately, and I did! The use of spanking must be tempered with love. An age-old African proverb states: "If one spanks a child with the right hand, one must also cuddle the child with the left hand." Translation: If you use corporal punishment to correct a misbehavior by your child, you should, not long after, cuddle the child and explain to him or her the reason for the punishment and why the behavior that caused the punishment is not acceptable and should not be repeated. Now, does it mean each time a child is spanked, the child must be cuddled immediately after? The answer is an emphatic NO! Just as spanking should not be used after each misbehavior, a parent ought to apply common-sense to determine when cuddling is appropriate.

> *Good judgement comes from experience, and experience ----- well, that comes from poor judgement.   - Unknown*

At this point, let us note some words of caution regarding the use of spanking. A parent MUST avoid spanking a child when the parent is angry. It does not matter the source of the anger. The parent may be very angry about the misbehavior of the child, or just angry about something else. It is when spanking is applied in anger that it may lead to unintended injury or abuse. This is a guiding principle that I adhered to judiciously. Let's face it! There are many things happening in the life of a parent other than a child's misbehavior. The child's misbehavior may, sometimes, compound the problem. In such cases, it is not advisable to spank a child immediately. I have been in such circumstances myself and each time, I always made a conscious effort not to punish the offending child immediately. It might have been a rough day at work, or I was experiencing some difficulties with my wife, a friend, a relative, and on top of that, a child misbehaves. What I have done in such circumstances was to tell the child, if corporal punishment was the most appropriate corrective measure, that the punishment for the misbehavior would be one, two, three, ten or twelve strokes of the cane, as the case maybe. However, that the child would be punished later. Of course, I made sure the punishment was actually carried out later!

The other cautionary note is that corporal punishment MUST be deliberate and intentional. That is, it must be applied to a specific part of the body in measured strokes. Spanking, for instance, implies 'strokes applied to the buttocks.' In my days of applying corporal punishment to my children, that was my favorite spot. Why? It is very effective and least prone to resulting in any injury to the child. Corporal punishment can also be applied to the palm of the hand. It could also be applied to the sole of the feet.

> *The test of a civilization is in the way it cares for its helpless members. - Pearl Buck*

All these parts of the body appear to be the least prone to serious injury.

Finally, it should be noted that there are other ways of punishing children other than the use of corporal punishment, and those other ways should also be used at different times. Some of those measures, like restricting them to their rooms, denying them favorite privileges, etc., have been mentioned earlier. However, based on my experience as a parent with a strong believe in traditional and religious values, it is my expert opinion that at the early stages of a child's development, even up to about the age of ten, corporal punishment is more effective than other forms of punishment, if used judiciously.

> *In the city of Pocatello, Idaho, the carrying of concealed weapons is forbidden, unless same are exhibited to public view. Also, it is prohibited for pedestrians and motorists to display frowns, grimaces, scowls, threatening and glowering looks, gloomy and depressed facial appearances, generally all of which reflect unfavorably upon the city's reputation. It's the law!*

CHAPTER 7

The Guilt Factor

M ost parents today grew up as children in an era of PLENTY. There seemed to be plenty of everything in the 'good old days', so to speak. There was plenty of money (relatively speaking), plenty of time, plenty of parental attention, plenty of trust, plenty of honesty, plenty of love, the list is endless!. There was so much plenty of everything that only one parent (mostly dads) had to work for families to make ends meet.

However, the 'old order' had changed. Nowadays, instead of plenty, there is scarcity of everything. As a matter of fact, for everything listed above as plenty in the past, there is now scarcity! Hence, it now takes two-income parents to maintain a family. Some parents even now need to have more than one full-time job to make ends meet. So, what parents cannot give emotionally, in terms of time, love and affection, they give materially. The little time given to children is now popularly referred to as "quality time".

As a result, modern society is now creating a group of children brought up under the influence of baby-sitters, day-care centers, television and, of course, invisible 'on-line' friends through the Internet. These latter group, the so-called 'on-line' friends are mostly disturbed and mentally unstable adults whose interactions with children can be very dangerous and even deadly. There have been true stories of such on-line friends who lured children with the promise of good times, by sending them travel tickets to meet them at some secret location. Some children have fallen for such traps and have met their untimely deaths in the process.

Children, especially teenagers, are increasingly lacking in moral and ethical values. The main problem is the lack of basic values being passed down from parents. Being a parent today seems harder than ever before. Thus, being a kid is even harder too. Teenagers are rude, irresponsible, selfish and wild. They seem to have too much time on their hands. Many teenagers are apt to claim that there are usually no adults at home when they return from school. Kids younger than teens are seen by adults as spoiled and disrespectful. They are indulged with material goods by guilty parents who do not spend enough time with them and do not enforce basic standards. It is common sight nowadays to see children who are out of control in public areas such as shopping centers, restaurants or the movies. The sages of ancient times likened *values* to *vaccines* and they are right. How so?. Well, if children are inoculated with appropriate values, they will be able to resist the world's many troubles and traps.

Parents should be sympathized with for feeling guilty or being blamed for this state of affairs. The current state of affairs should be put in the context of a world with failing public schools, spreading urban crime waive, degrading popular culture, demanding jobs and changing expectations. Both parents and teachers now see that their authority had been undermined, probably by each other, to some extent, and that the threat of litigation had severely diminished their ability to discipline children. At the same time, not many people are inclined to go back to the days of not sparing the rod. Love seems to be the popular answer nowadays. However, in the western world, especially in the United States of America, if affection does not help, police-imposed curfews and tougher punishments for those who commit crimes are seen as good ideas. This attitude, I beg to opine, is reflective of helplessness and the lack of will and guts by parents who refuse to take the proverbial "bull by the horns". In short, many parents are now looking up to the government to play the tough parental roles to keep the 'brats' in line.

In contemporary times, parents now want non-profit organizations such as the Boys or Girls Scouts and after-school programs to give children constructive things to do, with a moral underpinning. Some parents also want schools to do more than merely teaching academics. They want schools to do more in teaching basic values and enforcing discipline and work habits. There is a general belief that children want to be better, if only they were shown the way and given a chance. This, I believe, is a basic fact. However, I also believe that parents, and only parents, can show the way and give their children the chance to be better; not the schools and, definitely not day-care centers or non-profit organizations. According to the sages of old, "charity begins at home."

So, what can parents do to get out of this guilt trap? The following are the ten cardinal rules to follow:

1. Make your family, not work, your top priority.
2. Be generous with your time and attention to your children.
3. Listen, listen, listen, to your children.
4. Smile and hug your children often, but at least, twice daily.
5. Discipline your children positively, instantaneously and consistently.
6. Say "yes" when you can; say "no" when you must.

7. Admit your mistakes with dignity, letting your children know early that 'to err is human'.
8. Establish family routine so you can do things together as a family.
9. Make promises and keep them.
10. Slow down: allow time for resting, relaxing and just enjoying being in close proximity as a family.

Life is a picnic, but sometimes you have to pick up the blanket and use it as a tent.
- Unknown

CHAPTER 8

Community Role
In Parenting

T he first Lady of the United States during the Clinton presidency, Hillary Rodham Clinton, renewed the popularity of the age-old African proverb that states: "It takes a village to raise a child" in her book titled: "IT TAKES A VILLAGE *And Other Lessons Children Teach Us.*"[2] The book made the bestseller list instantly! The book highlighted the importance of the role of the community in raising a child properly. The book also chronicles Mrs.

---

[2]   *"It Takes A Village And Other Lessons Children Teach Us" was published by Simon & Schuster, Rockefeller Center, 1230 Avenue of the Americas, New York, NY 10020, U.S.A., 1996.*

Clinton's quest to discover how we can make our global society, in contemporary times, into the kind of village that enables children to grow into able, caring and resilient adults. At first, Mrs. Clinton's political adversaries, mostly conservative Republicans on the far right of the political spectrum, wanted to make light of the slogan by saying it takes a parent, not a village, to raise a child. But during the Democratic Party Convention in Chicago in 1996, Mrs. Clinton *shot* back by repeating the theme, with some further explanation, differentiating between the role of the parents and the community in the honorable task of raising a child.

The idea of the community role in the raising of a child can be traced back to Africa where the slogan was known to have first originated. Contrary to the ordinary interpretation that the detractors of the slogan may want to give it, the intent of the slogan was not, in anyway, to suggest that parents were expected to abandon their role of raising their children and leave the responsibility to the community. Rather, it is an acknowledgment that parents cannot do it alone. In ancient times, in African villages, all adults were supposed to, and took on the responsibility of overseeing the activities of children around them at any time of the day. The idea being that the children would grow up one day to become adults in the community. Hence, the need to pass on the traditional values of the community by maintaining constant and collective vigilance on the activities of the children, to ensure that they do the right things always, in terms of behavior in general.

The concept appears simple and straightforward. At least we have all been children before. It is customary for children to want to stray from the proper behavioral pattern taught them by their parents, once the parents are out of sight. However, once every adult in a community subscribes to the idea of exerting moral authority over a child, similar to that of a parent, it becomes difficult, if not impossible for children in that community to misbehave anywhere in the community, regardless of whether their parents are present or not. It is very important for the entire community to subscribe to the idea before it could work. It is also important for parents to follow up, with appropriate discipline, whenever an adult member of the community reports to them an observed misbehavior of their child outside the home.

I grew up in a relatively small and close-nit community. I was brought up the old-fashioned way. That is, respecting my parents and other people, particularly anybody older than me, whether within or outside of my community. Any adult in the community had the right to discipline any kid found misbehaving anywhere in the community. Depending on the gravity of the misbehavior, it might also be reported to one's parents, which, in those days, meant double jeopardy! Why? Because it meant that the child would also be disciplined again when he or she got home.

In my limited travels around the world, I have witnessed juvenile misbehavior in the presence of adults. I have always been amazed when adults just watch and look the other way on those occasions. The problems seem to be more prevalent in urban areas. Even in the so-called rural areas, it is becoming normal for adults to watch helplessly when youths misbehave in public. It appears the moral courage of adults to steer kids in the right direction has eroded over time. To gain it back, seems to me, very simple. All adults need, in my opinion, is to become themselves (again). It is amazing how responsive youths could be if an adult could summon enough courage to correct them when they are doing something that is either morally or ethically wrong. I have tried it and it has always worked for me! What I have found surprising is that many of these misbehaving youths do not know any better!

An example that really opened my eyes was when some teenagers were jumping over my fence as short-cuts to their apartments. I confronted one of them one day as he was about to do it in my presence. His response to me was that he did not see anything bad in what he was about to do as long as he was not going to hurt anyone by doing it. I swallowed hard, and took time to explain to him that jumping a fence was bad behavior in addition to being a violation of the law, also referred to as "trespassing." I concluded that while he might not be hurting anyone by doing it, it was still not a good way to behave. Whether the kid took it to heart or not, I could not tell. However, he was grateful for my advice and turned back toward the direction from which he came, and promised not to do it again. I have never seen him around my fence since then. But the main point of my story is that if other community adults can take the courage and time to talk to the likes of this kid on these and similar misbehavior, the community would not only be a better place to live, because of significant reduction in juvenile delinquencies, but the community adults would have contributed their quota in the raising of the community children.

> *Never one thing and seldom one person can make for a success. It takes a number of them merging into one perfect whole.*
> *- Marie Dressler*

CHAPTER 9

When Does A Child Outgrow Discipline?

T his is a somewhat rhetorical question. It is rhetorical because even though it looks so simple and loaded with a temptation to respond to it in a short, sweet and simple way, it does, in all reality, need a deep and thoughtful answer. However, if one remembers the adage: "he who pays the piper dictates the tune," answering this question becomes quite easy. Why? I am glad you asked!

A child can only be deemed to have fully outgrown discipline when the child does not, in any shade or form, rely on the parent for any need whatsoever. In other words, a child, regardless of how old, should still be subject to discipline as long as he or she still lives with the parents, or still has any financial dependence on the parents, regardless of how small or big. It is even more critical if both conditions apply to the child!

In most available literature on parenting, it is not uncommon to read that a child should not be subjected to child-like discipline any longer after they become teenagers. After attaining those 'magical' teenage years, they are deemed to have become aware of right and wrong, thus only needing limited guidance from parents henceforth in their lives. While this may be true about some children, my experience is that most children must continue to be subjected to disciplinary measures long after they become teenagers. In fact, as implied at the beginning of this chapter, disciplinary measures should stop only when a child is one hundred percent financially independent. One hundred percent financial independence means being out of the house and being responsible for their needs in totality. Except for extenuating circumstances, it is logical to assume that any adult, recognized by the society as such, who still lives with or depends on his or her parents for financial support, should never be left out of the disciplinary loop. As the saying goes, sometimes attributable to one of Murphy's Laws, "anything (or person) left alone can only go from bad to worse." Of course, disciplinary measures for an adult child are not expected to be the same as those for an adolescent child, while those for a teenager are also expected to be different from those for a toddler, etc. However, to provide a constant reminder to dependent children that maturity comes with self-dependency, it is important that some limits and rules are set for them and if those limits or rules are violated, some disciplinary measures should be instituted and applied.

Enough of the generalities! Let us examine some examples of limits and rules for an adult child who still resides with, and has some financial dependency on his or her parents. One of the most common areas of problems between adult children and their parents is the case of the adult child bringing their girlfriends or boyfriends home. There is nothing wrong with adult children bringing strangers home, or being visited by their friends of the opposite sex. However, depending on the moral, religious and cultural inclination of the parents, it may be problematic if the friends turn the parents' house into their second home, or even, their first home, in some cases. For most parents I know, including yours truly, it is totally unacceptable for adult children to be romantically entangled with their lovers in the parents' house, be it behind closed doors or not, as long as they are not married to each other. Here, we are talking of both traditional and religious discipline for the most part. This is a rule that the parents must set very firmly and up front for their adult child if the child wants to continue to reside with the parents. For parents who have raised a child up appropriately to that point, this rule would not be too foreign to the adult child. However, just like anything else, the parents must not relent in their enforcement of this rule, among others.

Another common area of problems with adult children living at home is keeping late nights-out. While parents must respect and provide some independence to their adult children, it is important for them to know why the adult children have to stay out late often. If it is job-related, it should be understandable. But when they are social nights-out, a parent must know and must regulate such habits to some extent. Why? For many reasons. For example, since evil usually lurks in dark places, a lot of bad people operate their bad deeds at night. Drug transaction comes readily to mind. Even though the child may not be involved in drugs, he or she, by roaming the streets at night, may become an innocent victim of a drug war between gangs or even war-lords! This example may be a 'stretch', but it is probable.

Another example of a potential problem between parents and children, regardless of age, is keeping their rooms clean, in particular, and providing appropriate assistance in keeping the house clean in general. Again, for an adult child, this should not pose too much problem if the child had been raised by the same parents all along, assuming house-cleaning was a discipline entrenched in the child's upbringing. However, part of the disciplinary routine is that parents must set rules for keeping the house clean in general. Breaking of such rules should be followed by some disciplinary measures. For an adult child, short of making them do the chores by force, a maid service could be hired at the expense of the child, when the cleaning rules are violated.

The types of disciplinary measures applicable to a child at different ages have been discussed in detail in a separate chapter and need not be repeated here. In fact, this chapter did not set out to discuss disciplinary measures. This chapter is about when a child could, or should outgrow discipline. Despite what some experts say, it is the considered and practical opinion of this author that a child should outgrow discipline only when that child has become a responsible adult, living outside of the parents' home and also maintaining one hundred percent financial independence.

We grow neither better nor worse as we get old, but more like ourselves.   - May Becker

CHAPTER 10

When Does A Child Become An Adult?

B iologically, a typical human being reaches adulthood between the ages of 20 and 40. This is the period universally accepted as the defining period for attaining young adulthood. It is the period when human beings make most of the decisions that will affect the rest of their lives. We are talking of decisions regarding their health, their happiness, and their success. In the western world, it is the stage of life when most people leave the parental home, take their first job, get married, have and raise children. From my life experience, and as corroborated by social scientists, it appears to be the most stressful years in the life span of a typical human being!

By the age of 20, most children worldwide, under normal circumstances, would have completed, at least, one year of post-secondary school education. For most children in the western world, it means an average of two years of college or university life is already completed. This is the age when they are thinking of the career path they want to create through the major areas of academic endeavors they want to pursue. Obviously, children at this age (that is age of 20) are still maturing in many important ways. These arbitrarily defined years (20-40) hold great potential for the furtherance of intellectual, emotional and physical development. Generally, it is about this time in life we, as human beings, start to assume new roles in our personal lives. We become workers, spouses, and subsequently, parents. These roles, according to Dianne E. Papalia and Sally Wendkos Olds, in their book, Human Development, affect the way we think and the way we act. The way we think and act affects the way we carry out these roles, if we carry them out at all.

As discussed in philosophical literature, when a human being reaches maturity, or when a human being has procreated, or are able to procreate, the physical life cycle is completed insofar as it involves that human being. Life is entirely indifferent to whether a person succeeds or not. Life is indifferent as to whether one experiences suffering or happiness. Pythagoras compared life to the great games, such as the Olympics. He said some went to the games to compete for prizes; others went there just to sell their wares as vendors; but the best of all were those who became spectators of the games. The spectator of life is one who has a philosophical attitude. The spectator of life does not presume that life has any single value to anybody. He or she believes there are a variety of values, thus participating in as many experiences as possible.

Pythagoras divided life into four quarters, each of twenty years. The first quarter is the boyhood or girlhood period. The second quarter is youth. The third quarter is young adulthood; and the fourth quarter, old adulthood. These four quarters correspond to the four seasons of the year; namely, boyhood or girlhood to Spring, youth to Summer, young adulthood to Autumn, and old adulthood to the Winter season.

Another great philosopher, Henry Cornelius Agrippa, in his renowned work, *The Magic Mirror*, also divided life into four quarters. The first quarter, he relates, is from the first to the twenty-first year. It is the Spring season of the life and represents youth, love, and growth. The second quarter is from the age of twenty-two to forty-two. It is the Summer period. It represents mind, intellect, maturity of thought, manhood or womanhood, fruitage or accomplishment. The third quarter, covering the years from forty-three to sixty-three, the fall season of life, he depicts as wealth, physical and mental maturity and karma[3]. The fourth and last, or Winter season, includes the years from sixty-four to eighty-four, and is the time of the Passover, or the preparation for death. Each of these quarters of life, he stated, begins with the Vernal Equinox, the Spring period, and each of the quarters of life ends at the Winter Solstice, (which, in nature, is about December 21). Agrippa also related that a human being has three equal points in life. In other words, there are three periods within life and these three periods he referred to as being primary initiations which we must pass through during our life period. The first begins after birth, the first

---

[3]   *Karma is a term used to mean the working of the law of compensation. In layman's terms, Karma is, simply, a natural law of cause and effect. That is, for every action, there is an equal and opposite reaction. One of the fundamental principles of the law of compensation is that for each sorrow or joy we cause another, we shall have experiences in like degree and manner and at times when the lessons to be gained thereby will be the most impressive. This principle does not exact an eye for an eye or a life for a life, for there is no vengeance in the process, and no intention to cause suffering. The sole purpose of Karma is to teach us the lesson, to make us realize our errors and to evolve the understanding thereby.*

Spring quarter of our life, from one to twenty-one years of age. The second period comes at forty-eight years of age, when we have crossed the meridian of life, or the zenith of our life's period; and the third period, when we enter into the Winter season of our life, the sunset, the closing quarter.

Agrippa analyzes most interestingly the value of these seasons or quarters of life, and what a person is expected to do in order to utilize them intelligently. By the time one has attained twenty-one years of age and has completed the Spring season of life, one should then have received the *tools* for one's future. These tools may be the trade or profession in which one should be trained or prepared, or they may consist of the accumulated experiences of others which were expounded to the person by preceptors in schools or universities. The Summer season of life, the middle period, is the time for activity, mental and physical. It is a time to produce; namely, to create and manifest the ideals which should have been established during the Spring season of life. The Winter season, or the sunset years, states Agrippa, is the time to reap the benefits, if any, from what has preceded. That is, it is the time we should begin to enjoy the results of thoughtful planning or living, or when we should experience the results of careless living and wasted years.

So, when does a child become an adult? From the foregoing, it appears the universally accepted age of adulthood is twenty-one. In most western countries, that is the average age that college or university kids finish their junior (or third) year. Thus, having only one more year remaining for the completion of their university education. Without trying to repeat the life-cycle explanation given above, it is clear that up until the age of twenty-one, children need all of the guidance and direction they can get from their parents. This information cannot be stressed enough because there is a central tendency for parents to want to 'hands-off' their kids as soon as they enter the university. As a matter of fact, most kids prefer it that way and go to great extent to carry themselves as such. Based on my experience with my college-age children, it is only a *front*! These children need, and can use all the guidance they can get until, at least, they become twenty-one years old. Since the fingers of our hands are not equal, it should be noted that some kids mature faster and may be capable of attaining independence earlier. The fact of the matter is, most kids do need, and can use the guidance!

Silence is the best tactic for him who distrusts himself.   - La Rochefoucauld
Experience keeps a dear school, but fools will learn in no other.   - Benjamin Franklin

Before you finally go ahead and have children, find a couple who are already parents and berate them about their methods of discipline, lack of patience, appallingly low tolerance levels, and how they have allowed their children to run riot. Suggest ways in which they might improve their child's sleeping habits, toilet training, table manners and overall behavior. Enjoy it! - It'll be the last time in your life that you will have all the answers.   *- Unknown*

Life appears to be too short to be spent in nursing animosity or registering wrong.
                    - Charlotte Bronte

CHAPTER 11

Parenting Teenagers

T he teenage years are about the most complex formative years of a human being. It appears that is why, universally, teenagers are about the most difficult group of children for adults to deal with. First, to put the issue of *parenting teenagers* in perspective, it is appropriate to repeat here where teenagers fall in the *Quarters of Life*. As stated in the previous chapter (*Chapter 10*), the great philosopher, Henry Cornelius Agrippa, in his renowned work, *The Magic Mirror*, divided life into four quarters. The first quarter, he relates, is from the first to the twenty-first year. It is the Spring of life and represents youth, love and growth.

The other three quarters, Summer, Fall and Winter, are also described in details in the previous chapter (*Chapter 10*). The first quarter, Spring, is the quarter of relevance in this chapter because it is in this quarter that the teenage years of life reside.

By the time one has attained twenty-one years of age and has completed the Spring season of life, Agrippa believed that one should then have received the tools for one's future. These tools may be the trade or profession in which one should be trained or prepared, or they may consist of the accumulated experiences of others which were expounded to the person by preceptors in schools or universities, or in this case, parents.

The teenage years are usually the most difficult ones in the parent-child relationship because these are the years of separation. Both parent and child are experiencing challenges in their individual personal development. The child is learning how to function as an independent adult which means that he or she must move away from the home environment physically, emotionally and psychologically. The parent is learning to let go. The process requires that both the parent and child learn to live with ambiguity, complexity and compromise at all levels of interaction.

The teenage years are necessarily challenging, but if the challenge is embraced with a whole heart and an open mind, there is the potential for profound personal growth and the joy of developing abiding friendship between parent and child. There are three powerful fears that often interfere with a parent's ability to solve the problems of parenting teenagers.

The first fear arises from a natural instinct of parents to guide and protect. Parents often fear that children will be hurt, will make mistakes, or will somehow not be able to cope with life's challenges.

As an example, just recently, I was visited by a parent (a very close family friend) who drove her daughter - a second-year college student majoring in pharmacy, to her first job (a summer internship). Her daughter was to start the summer internship the following day and the mother wanted to show her daughter how to drive to the job without getting on the interstate highway. Why? Because she (the mother) feared driving on the interstate highways herself. So, she did not want her daughter (who is twenty-one years old!) "exposed" to the "danger" of driving on major highways. In the poor lady's presence, I asked the daughter if she was afraid of driving on the interstate highways, her response was a resounding "NO".

If we examine this fear for our children honestly, we will find that, as evident in the example cited, it is rooted in our own fear of being hurt, of making mistakes, or of not being able to cope. A parent's task as guide and protector, is to support and encourage a child's natural instinct to explore, to experiment, to risk, and to grow. This is done by making many choices and by default, responsibilities, available to the teenager in all spheres of life. Setting guidelines often generates conflict because the teenager is learning to appreciate the balance between choice and responsibility while the parent is learning to make new choices that limit his or her sense of responsibility. Both are required to change their perceptions of the relationship because the interaction patterns are changing as part of a natural developmental process.

> *In quiet places, reason abounds.*
> *- Adlai Stevenson*

As parents, we set the tone of this process by our conscious awareness that it is happening in the first place; by continual self-examination of our own motives and emotional response; by establishing values of honest communication and mutual respect through personal example. The more we learn to trust our own growth process, the more we learn to trust our teenager's ability to meet his or her own life challenges.

The second fear is rooted in a parent's confusion about where the parent fits into the world around him or her, that is, the parent's public identity. Both the parent and the teenager are vulnerable to peer pressure until they learn to accept responsibility for self. This is a difficult issue to resolve at any age and in any circumstance. When we are deeply emotionally involved, we become vulnerable to each other in significant ways. Often we feel we are vulnerable to what other people will think about us because of what someone close to us is doing. We know as adults that this is an illusion because true relationships are honest and supportive. Here, we are essentially talking about group consciousness and our natural interdependence as human beings.

If we, as parents, become involved in a situation where we feel that our reputation is jeopardized by our teenager's behavior, it is extremely important that we immediately examine our own fears. If we are relating to our child as if he or she is a reflection of ourself, and therefore what he or she does affects our reputation, we have given our child too much power in our relationship, thus denying the child his or her own personality or identity. The more narrow-minded we are, the more we will try to restrict our teenager's life experience, often with drastic consequences, open rebellion, and conflict. Parents should avoid the temptation to force a child (especially a teenager) to live up to the parents' expectations all the time. The child will instinctively resist either openly or passively, because of the threat such parental control poses on the child's natural growth process. Parents must give up their own fears in order to re-open communication with their teenager.

If our adult relationships are truly jeopardized by our teenager's behavior, it is time to reevaluate those relationships as well as our relationship with our child. Human diversity celebrates difference for it is a reflection of the power of the creative imagination, of the individuation process, and of the potential for personal development.

The third fear -- the fear of not being loved, affects both the parent and the teenager, although parents are less apt to recognize it in themselves. We fear that we will not be understood, that we will be rejected, that we will not be believed -- all the fears we suffered from at the same age and have not resolved as adults. This is a particularly important fear to look at - the fear of not being loved, in relationship to parenting teenagers. The developmental process requires that the parent-child connection be deliberately loosened but not broken, that the parent and child learn to be friends, to recognize and respect each other's individuality. Since this is a gradual process extending over several years with inevitable conflicts, interaction and communication must be approached with care. Parenting teenagers successfully requires courage, concentration, and commitment to one's own personal growth process. The teenage years are filled with change for both the parent and the child. Change can be experienced as exciting and challenging, or as fearful and overwhelming. The key is found near our own hearts, in our capacity to love, to give as we would receive. The fear of not being loved is overcome when we love without thought of self or the need for love returned.

This is particularly true as parents when we expect or demand that our children understand and appreciate "all that we have done for them." In reality, that understanding and appreciation usually comes after the child has become an adult!

> *Maturity is only a short break in adolescence.*
> *- Jules Feiffer*

> *No one is exempt from talking nonsense; the*
> *only misfortune is to do it solemnly.   - Rene*
> *Montaigne (a 19th century philosopher)*

> *In the State of Georgia, U.S.A., all males*
> *between the ages of 16 and 50 are required to*
> *work on public roads. In Quitman, Georgia,*
> *it is illegal for a chicken to cross a road. It's*
> *the law!*

CHAPTER 12

Sibling Rivalry: What Can Parents Do?

S ibling rivalry is one inevitable phenomenon that rears its ugly head in some shape or form in every family where there are two or more kids. It is more prevalent when kids are not too far apart in age, say somewhere between one to five years in age differences. In most families, it usually starts when there is a new baby. The older kid, noticing a loss of attention to him or her, and a flurry of attention to the new baby, naturally gets envious of the baby, and if vocal enough, would admonish the parents to take the new baby back to the hospital or wherever the baby came from. If the older kid is not the verbal type, some passive-aggression could be noticeable instantly and may be directed towards the new baby. The onus is on the parents, at such critical point in the relationship formation between the two siblings, to assure the older child that he or she is still loved and cared about. In fact, it helps a lot if the mother can involve the older kid, as much as is practicable, in the care of the new baby.

When siblings are old enough to become playmates, parents must pay particular attention to any traits of sibling rivalry and step in as soon as they develop. Children seven years old and younger tend to be very individualistic in nature and would go to any length to protect their individuality without any regard to the feelings or rights of their sibling, or anybody else for that matter. They can use any means at their disposal, including violence, to achieve their objective. Parents must step in as appropriate, to set boundaries and establish appropriate rules of behavior. Since boys tend to resort to violence more quickly than girls, parents must protect the interests and safety of the girls more, while at the same time, maintaining balance, neutrality and fairness. It is important that parents not take sides at such times. Disciplinary measures must be applied especially to deter fighting or any other form of violence. Appropriate measures in such circumstances include, but not limited to: 1) loss of privileges and 2) spending time in their rooms.

My first two children, Tim and Debbie are exactly two years apart, in age. They both grew up to be very much fond of each other up to the time they both reached seven and five years old, respectively. While there were minor fights between them up until that time, the fights were not too problematic or frequent. The rivalry really blossomed when Tim started school and started having other playmates! Then, he did not want Debbie hanging around him anymore! Not even touch his toys!! As expected, Tim started hitting Debbie at every opportunity. Noticing this, I told both of them to ensure that they report each other to either me or their mother whenever there was a disagreement. Knowing that Tim was more aggressive, being the MALE, I ordered him to always ensure that he did not hit Debbie first and in case Debbie hit him first, to not hit her back but first report her to me or their mother. This latter instruction turned out to be a mistake! Why? Debbie, armed with the knowledge that Tim would not hit her back, became the aggressor and felt very free and empowered to hit Tim at any instance. Tim turned out to be the 'wimp' between the two of them. This was a mistake that I would advise all parents reading this book to avoid. The lesson here is that girls can be aggressive too, given the right circumstance! As of the time of writing this book, Tim and Debbie are twenty and eighteen years old, respectively, lead two separate and different lives, have little or no communication whatsoever, and would rather not have anything to do with each other. Did we, or are we doing anything about this? Of course we did and we are!! They, too, are aware of the awkwardness of the situation. As a matter of fact, during Tim's freshman year in college, he made a special telephone call home and talked at length with Debbie about their relationship and how he wants to have a more loving brother-sister relationship with her. Debbie replied in kind. However, as of the time of finalizing this chapter of the book, which is late summer 1998, less than one week before Tim starts his junior year in college, and Debbie starts her freshman year in the same college, their relationship, as outwardly apparent, still appears *as cool as a cucumber*! Translation: They are still *cold* towards each other and try, as much as possible, to avoid each other at every opportunity! It should be recalled that Tim has been home since college closed for the end of the 1997-1998 academic year, which was since mid-May, 1998! Hence, if there was any time to improve the relationship, there have been plenty of time and opportunity! It is sad to note that they are both 'set' in their 'coldness' toward each other, no matter what their mother and I may do to influence any positive change. My wife and I discuss it a lot. We put almost equal amount of blame on both of them, while accepting our share of the blame for not doing a good parental job, in this regard, in the first place. Anyway, we have resolved not to give up but to keep working on the problem for as long as it takes.

What is the moral of this experience? Parents should not stand by and watch helplessly as sibling rivalry rages between (or among) their children. While acknowledging that parents can only do so much (as is evident in our experience), it is still imperative that parents try their best to mediate fairly, and if possible, develop a workable solution. It may work out and it may not. However, I know one thing for sure. As long as parents try their best, even if does not appear to work out instantly, just trying has some impact and goes a long way in helping the children get along better, down the road.

Prejudice: a vagrant opinion without visible means of support.   - Ambrose Bierce

CHAPTER 13

Case Studies

The focus of this chapter is on particular real life incidents between parents and children observed by the author. First, the incidents are presented as they actually occurred, then the author's opinion is presented immediately after the narration of each incident.

Scenario 1: At an ongoing soccer game between two fifth and sixth-grade combined teams (9-12 year olds), a mother arrived late and had to walk across the field to the spectators' stand designated for the parents for her team. Actually, this lady did not have a child on any of the two soccer teams. She was there because she was the assistant coach for one of the teams. She briskly walked around the field, making sure she was as far away behind the goal post as possible. Following her was her daughter, who, I would guess, was about four years old. The little girl, instead of following in her mother's path, decided to take a short cut and walked straight across the field, thus interrupting the on-going game. She made it across alright, and the game continued despite her intruding presence. I had been waiting for the assistant coach myself to ask her a few questions regarding the team's after-game pizza party, since that was the last game for the Fall soccer season. So, I followed her briskly around the field. I caught up with her at the same time her daughter reached her after interrupting the game. As soon as the girl reached her mother, and before I could ask her my question, she gave the girl a stern rebuke about her "rude" and "unruly" behavior for crossing the field that way. After rebuking her sufficiently, she explained to her why her behavior was not appropriate, and why she, herself, had to approach the spectators' stand by walking around the field instead of crossing it. From the look on the little girl's face, she felt sorry for what she did and surely understood her mother's point.

Comment: The mother's reaction was very appropriate, timely and effective. Corrective measures are most effective when they are instant and delivered with authority as rightly done by this mother. Based on the little girl's reaction, it was obvious that this mother had always exercised parental authority and control over her daughter. The moral of this story is twofold: First, an erring child must be corrected instantly regardless of whether the misdeed caused any harm or not. Second, the tone during the delivery of the corrective measures must be stern, albeit not necessarily loud, to be effective. This mother clearly did both!

Scenario 2:   I was at another soccer game, this time between two third-grade teams (7 and 8-year olds). It was about twenty minutes before the game. The coach for my son's team had not yet arrived. So, I was standing in the company of other "early-bird" parents awaiting the arrival of the coach for our children's team. Well, as expected, the 7 and 8-year olds could not just stand around doing nothing like the parents. So, what did they do? Some of them were kicking the soccer ball to each other, which was okay. However, the others started to climb the gates of the fence around the soccer field, swinging the gates back and forth, while they all hung on. Noting that one of them might fall down and get hurt, one of the parents asked them to stop. He implored them as gently as he could as follows: "Don't climb the gate please. Eric, Robert, stop climbing and swinging the gate.....pleeeeease." The kids did not pay any attention to him. I wanted to repeat what he said in a more commanding tone that, I believe the kids would have understood. I did not, because my son was not among those climbing the gate. This particular parent was imploring them to stop because his son was among them. The other two parents, who also had children among those climbing the gate, did not utter any word. So, I kept my trap shut. Since the kids seemed to be having fun with this potentially dangerous game and did not heed the appeal from this parent, he tried one more time, in the same tone as before. Sure, enough, and before he finished his appeal, one of the kids fell down and was hit by the swinging gate. That kid was his son, Eric! Of course, Eric was sprawling on the ground, wreathing in pain, crying. So, the poor dad, after reminding him of his prior warning for them to stop, had no choice but to pick Eric up and massage and console him.

Comment: This parent's error seems obvious! To the uninitiated, his main error was that he did not ask the children to stop in a stern tone that children of that age could have understood. In my opinion, this parent was caught up in the mentality of being civil to children, while at the same time, trying to make them do things that are necessary for their own good! All that parent should have said was: "Okay, I want you all to stop climbing that gate right now. I mean, everybody, come down right now." It is my experience that those kids would have responded to that tone. Then, after they might have complied, one could go over and briefly explain to them the potential danger inherent in what they were doing.

Scenario 3: I was at a baseball game in which my eleven year-old son, Bobby, was playing. There was a concession stand in operation at the game. Shortly before the end of the game, which was around 10:00 p.m., because it was the last game of the day, one of the players approached his mother to make a request. The mother was sitting in the spectators' stand next to me, where all anxious parents were waiting impatiently for the game to end. Why impatiently? Well, it was getting late into the evening on a weekday and we all needed to get up early the following morning to go to work! The boy asked his mother for money to go and buy something to eat at the concession stand. The mother was reluctant to give him money for two reasons. First, the game was almost over and they would soon be able to go home where the boy could eat whatever he wanted at much less cost. Secondly, the poor woman did not have much money in her purse, and probably had other plans for the little money she had. She tried to persuade her son against the idea for these two reasons. The boy persisted on his request and tried shedding some "crocodile" tears, pleading the fact that he was really hungry. Filled with the 'milk' of motherly compassion, the woman obliged and gave the boy the money.

As the boy left to buy the hot-dog sandwich, the woman started complaining loudly to the rest of the parents there, hoping to arouse some sympathy about what her "stubborn" son just did. No parent said a word! When the boy came back, the woman asked if she had any change back from the money she gave her, the boy said no. Then came a second loud complaint from the woman about how expensive the concession stand snack was. It was only his son who responded in the affirmative; everybody else pretended not to see or hear anything!

Comment: Obviously, this parent had raised this child to always get his way and the boy knew exactly what to do each time to let his parent give him whatever he wanted. It should be noted that allowing a child to go about with an empty stomach is not what is being suggested here. It is a basic parental responsibility to ensure that a child is fully and appropriately fed at all times. However, at the same time, a parent should also be able to say NO and stick with it when it is reasonable to do so. This was a classic example of such a case. After all, the child already ate dinner before coming to the game. This was the last game of the day which always started at 7:30 p.m. and always lasted about two and half hours. Even if the child was really hungry, it was not proper for him to eat a sandwich when the game in which he was participating was still going on. A fact known to him and his mother! Secondly, the game was soon going to be over and being a neighborhood league, nobody lived beyond fifteen minutes' drive from the venue of the game. Hence, asking the child to wait for another fifteen or twenty minutes before he could have something to eat, was not too much for a parent to ask. Finally, it was obvious, this woman was neither prepared nor willing to part with the little amount of money she had in her possession. I often wonder why parents easily give in as soon as their kid starts crying or shows a sign of teary eyes. Parents should remember that if their child did not cry in the hospital at birth, the child would have been regarded as still-born and would not have been released by the hospital as a well-baby. Hence, crying should not be a criterion for a child to have his or her way over the parent's objection.

The lessons one could learn from these case studies can be summarized as follows:

1.   An erring child must be corrected instantly regardless of whether the misdeed caused any harm or not.

2.   The tone during the delivery of corrective measures must be stern, albeit not necessarily loud, to be effective.

3.   A parent should be able to say NO to a child and stick with it when it is reasonable to do so.

4.   Parents should always resist the temptation to easily give in as soon as their kid starts crying or shows a sign of teary eyes. In other words, crying should not be a criterion for a child to have his or her way over the parent's objection.

What the mind conceives, humanity will eventually achieve. - Validivar

Every educated person should know a little of everything and something well.
            - A. Lawrence Lowell
        Harvard University's 22nd President

CHAPTER 14

Reflections

The parenting experience, while at times, arduous, is very pleasant and rewarding. I ought to know, having been a parent for about two decades! In addition to being a fulfillment of every human being's naturally ordained life mission, it is also an experience that neither formal education nor money can provide. It is a process by which God, acting through one human being, plans, shapes, forms, nurtures and directs the life of another human being in the right direction. It is an act every human being must meditate upon immensely before embarking on. It is a process that no human being can undertake alone. One requires divine guidance as well as full participation of the adults in one's community.

Having said all these, can one infer that every adult can, and should become parents at some point in one's life? While it is a laudable venture for every adult to aspire to undertake, the answer is an emphatic NO! It has been my experience that not all adults are *cut out* to be parents. Mediocrity begets mediocrity, states an age-old saying. In my humble opinion, bringing up an offspring is the most important contribution a human being can make to humanity. The continuity of life as we know it, depends on procreation. After procreation, the resulting children must be nurtured to become responsible and productive adults. That is where parenting comes in. Recall, that a parent is the adult who brings up a child regardless of whether or not the adult is biologically connected to the child! That is why any adult who cannot perform parenting duties, as sacredly as the process requires, should avoid either making babies, or even venturing into becoming a parent. As a matter of fact, such an adult would do humanity more good than harm by not becoming a parent in any shape or form.

Through the Divine Grace of God, I have managed to bring up four wonderful children of my own. They have stood up as good products of God's creation wherever they have been in life, so far. I am greatly indebted to God and to the communities in which I have resided over the years, for making my children turn out the way they have been perceived by others. This book did not set out to be a "be-all-and-end-all" in parenting. Please take it as an experience of one parent over time. If by any chance, you, the reader, has learned anything useful and helpful from it, please pass the word out so other parents, or would-be parents can benefit. May God bless you!

> *The tree of liberty requires watering with the sweat of patriots, else a time will come when only the blood of patriots can allow liberty to survive. - J. Melville Caps*

CHAPTER 15

Life's A Trip

There is no more befitting way to end this book than through a poem written in one of the reflective moments in the life of the author. The poem is about life, in general, but interspersed with lessons the author learned from his mother.

I was born into this world
Full of hope and empty of woe.
As I continue my life-long trip,
My hopes started dwindling,
My woes started growing.
Little did I know,
That of all the things in life,
Hope is not guaranteed,
Woes are more easily attained.
Which reminds me constantly
What my mother use to say.

My mother taught me to trust,
More than I can hope for.
The more trust I give,
The more woes I get.
Of all the woes I yet have gotten,
It seems clear to me over time,
That the most pain usually comes,
From trusted but untrusting souls,
Who reap from where they sow not,
And sow only where they can reap from.
So, hear ye all friends,
Life may be "a walking shadow" alright,
But it could also be a treat.
All it takes is a good mind,
A good attitude sure helps too,
To make life such a trip!

*We are here to add what we can to, not get
what we can from life.   - Sir William Osler*

Appendix

Parenting Resources

The following information is provided as additional resource for readers who may be interested in more information on parenting, for a variety of reasons. The listing is not intended to be exhaustive, by any means, but it provides links and references to other informational materials, thus making it invaluable to a reasonable extent. Most of the reference materials provided can be found in your local library. For readers who do not have Internet access at home, many public libraries in the U.S.A. now provide Internet access for public use.

Parenting Organizations & Support Groups

http://www.attachmentparenting.org
Attachment Parenting International
We strongly believe that attachment parenting methods not only strengthen families but provide a uniquely simple and cost-effective model to aid in the prevention of child abuse, behavioral disorders, criminal acts, and other serious social problems.

http://www.positiveparenting.com
POSITIVE PARENTING (ON-LINE!)
Welcome to Positive Parenting, dedicated to providing resources and

information to make parenting rewarding, effective and fun! We have classes and workshops in Ventura County . For parenting classes in your state, please visit our expert index.

http://www.4dad.com
Dad, find organizations, parenting & child support information Dads and dads-to-be will find all the parenting resources they need at 4Dad.com. Our researchers have spent hours researching the web to deliver this parenting web site. From celebratory cigars and birth announcements, to parental help and father organizations, you'll find it at 4Dads.

http://www.solo.org
Solo Parenting Alliance. Solo Parenting Support

http://www.med.jhu.edu/peds/neonatology
PEDIATRIC POINTS OF INTEREST
The Pediatric Points of Interest are a huge collection of pediatric (paediatric) links to child health, pediatrics, parenting, disease and illness, medical information for children, adolescents and babies related resources. The targeted audience are pediatric health care providers like pediatricians, family physicians, nurses, respiratory therapists, speech therapists and physical therapists.

http://sunsite.unc.edu/cheryb/women/wresources.html
Women's Resources:
There is a variety of information by and about women on the Internet. Here are a few things we have found: Browse All Sites by Title: A-L M-Z   Women's Resources on the Internet   Bisexual and Lesbian Resources

http://www.supportworks.org
Single Parenting Support Groups, Charlotte, NC. SupportWorks - directory of support groups and other resources in Charlotte, NC

addressing Single Parenting.

http://www.ez-guide.com/advice.htm
EZ-Guide: Experts & Advice: Financial, Advisors, Stocks, Bonds, Investments, Health, Medical, Law, Support Groups, Parenting - A guide to top, award winning, useful sites of experts in the fields of medicine, health, law, stocks and bonds, finances, consumers and advice on etiquette, parenting and support groups for many needs.

http://www.single-fathers.org
The Single and Custodial Fathers' Network is a virtual organization with membership through out the world linked together by the resources of the World Wide Web. The network includes both single and custodial fathers and is open to anyone.

http://parenthoodweb.com
ParenthoodWeb -- Parenting, Pregnancy, Family, Child care, Breast-feeding and Infant / Baby resources. The award-winning online parenting, pregnancy and family community for parents and prospective parents. Free expert advice, discussion groups & chat, polls, etc.

http://www.athenenet.co.uk/homepages/AndyGill
Practical Parenting - tips on common child behavior problems. Also research findings, advice and support to professionals wanting to run effective parenting groups.

http://www.fcs.wa.gov.au
Family and Children's Services, Western Australia - Family and Children's Services aims to advance the general well-being of Western Australian families, individuals and groups within our community.

http://www.vaughan-vaughan.com
Vaughan-Vaughan Home Page - Resources by Peggy Vaughan and

James Vaughan, Ph.D. regarding extramarital affairs, Beyond Affairs Network, life-planning, lasting love, and parenting/sex education.

http://tapestrybooks.com/parent/parindex.html
Tapestry Books - Parenting Challenges Resources - PARENTING CHALLENGES RESOURCES Where to get more information ONLINE Resources on Internet and the web PRINTED MATERIAL Magazines, newsletters, etc. ORGANIZATIONS Professional groups, support groups, etc; Tapestry Books

http://www.babyplace.com
THE BABY AND CHILD PLACE PARENTING HOME PAGE - Member of the Internet Link Exchange Where Parents Can Go To Find Everything They Want To Help Care For Their Children E-Mail us * Send us letters* Call us ATTENTION HUSH-A-BYE SHOPPERS, IMPORTANT INFO!! 'Passionate About Parenting' By Marnie.

http://www.mentor-media.com
Parenting on the Go: "Seek outside relationships" part 2 - Consider sources of support - Consider sources of support Does your child need help learning to get along with others? If so, consider the following sources of support: A school group run by counselors Boy or girl scouts Church groups Special interest groups, like chess clubs.

http://thefamilycenter.home.mindspring.com
The Family Center - "Offering family support services to meet the challenges of parenting in today's complex world." The Exchange Club Family Center for Alamance County is a private nonprofit agency, created by concerned community members.

http://208.215.168.143
The National Parenting Center - Founded in July of 1989, The National Parenting Center (TNPC) has become one of America's foremost parenting information services. Dedicated to providing parents with

comprehensive and responsible guidance from nine of the world's most renowned experts.

http://www.kidtemp.com
Temperament Learning Center - offers temperament assessments, consultations, workshops, support groups, and classes developed to promote the understanding of temperament. We help professionals, educators and parents incorporate temperament concepts.

http://www.wordnet.co.uk/positive.htm
Positive Parenting - Registered Charity Number 1053361 Company Number 3162747 All the materials contained in these pages are the copyright of Positive Parenting Publications. Original cartoons by Sarah-Ann Wakeley Return to WordNet Good family life depends upon.

http://www.allofboulder.com/support.htm
Support Groups - Alliance For The Mentally Ill Of Boulder County 1333 Iris Avenue Boulder, CO 80304-2226 (303) 443-4591 Parenting Place 2222 14 Boulder, CO 80302-4822 (303) 449-0177 PFLAG Boulder 3827 Angelovic Court Boulder, CO 80301.

http://www.pgi.edu/cfccgrps.htm
CFCC Support Groups - Descriptions of Support Groups California Family Counseling Center; Phillips Home Page. CFCC offers a wide range of support groups: Children Relationships Communication Training Teen Group Adult Survivors.

http://church-of-christ.org/lists
Christian Discussion Groups - For Members of the Churches of Christ. We welcome your participation in the following ListServ Discussion Groups. This is an opportunity to fellowship with Christians worldwide. We pray that the Lord continue to bless.

http://www.familyville.com/data/bbs/Parenting
Parenting issues of any kind. Parenting God's Way Generously
sponsored by: Click graphic to visit them. Discussion Groups Children:
Parenting issues for people with young children. General Parenting:
General discussions about parenting.

http://www.seflin.org/parent
Parenting and Families - General Parenting Resources Adolescent &
Child Services Educating Parents / Educating Children Fathers Health
Issues Breast-feeding Nutrition Adoption Discipline/Behavior Child
care Safety Consumer.

Parenting Magazines/Newsletters

http://www.kjsl.com/parenting.html
Mailing List A support; information email forum for full time moms or
dads parenting in ways that promote attachment between parent and
child. Beyond One Year is the newsletter for anyone who enjoys
breast-feeding a toddler or older child and would like to hear about
other women who feel the same.

http://www.motherstuff.com
Parenting Links - Motherstuff
Baby Net: Tender Loving Care (TLC) General stuff. Baby Planner -
FamilyNet Internet Librarian Birth and Baby Planning NetBook -
Family Software A collection of parenting resources on the net.

http://www.kcts.org/product/single/RESOURCE.HTM
Research has shown that creating positive bonds with family members,
teachers and other adults protect children who are at risk for violent
behavior. Strong families who teach their children healthy beliefs and
set clear standards of behavior are most successful at raising children

who are resistant to negative forces in society.

http://www.sol.com
Dedicated to providing parents with comprehensive and responsible guidance from nine of the world's most renowned child-rearing authorities, The National Parenting Center invites parents to expand their parenting skills and strengths." Lisa Wilberding's Home Page A list of good sites: Pregnancy & Childbirth -- Babies On The Web -- Moms & Dads -- Breast-feeding Resources -- Medical Resources.

http://www.angelfire.com
PARENTING IN THE 90s
A site TOTALLY dedicated to Parents and those with children in their lives!

http://www.mcs.net/~kathyw/parent.html
Kathy's Essential Information for Parents

http://www.healthforums.com
Children The Challenge by Rudolf Dreikurs, M.D. with Vicki Soltz, R.N. The Parents Handbook by Don Dinkmeyer and Gary D. McKay. D. How To Talk So Kids Will Listen and Listen So Kids Will Talk by Adele Faber and Elaine Mazlish
Link to resources for special parenting situations.

http://www.en-parent.com
The Entreprenurial Parent.   Work-at-Home Mom Pro for Moms Online; e-mail: RobertsLMR@aol.com; P.O. Box 320722, fairfield, CT 06432. Tel: (203) 372-4977; Fax: (203) 371-6212.

http://www.kcts.org/product/single/tip8.htm
Helping your child prepare for the working world.   Supporting your child's spiritual development.

http://www.thefathersgroup.org
the Boston Parents Paper: 617-522-1515, Great coverage of local and state issues. Healthy Kids: 212-462-3300, How to raise physically healthy and emotionally developed children.

http://members.aol.com/ljdbush/recommended_reading_on_parenti ng.htm
Recommended Reading on Parenting:
With the same accessible style as How to Talk So Kids Will Listen (above), Faber and Mazlish tackle sibling relationships. If you're tired of the same old, same old advice from the mainstream parenting magazines, check this one out.

http://www.motherstuff.com/html/bibliography-pbook.htm
The Paper Pages - Parenting - Motherstuff
MaryHelen Lewis She's put together a bibliography of children's books with strong female role models! School Is Dead: Home schooling Resource Guides and How-to Books on Home schooling Extensive.

http://www.geocities.com/Heartland/1710/baby.htm
PARENTING RESOURCE CENTER has parenting Info.
Your membership in The Baby Sav-More Club includes a free hard copy newsletter that currently list over 100 freebies for infants and parents to take advantage of. To join the Baby Sav-More Club, please send name, address and only $5.00 to cover membership and postage/handling: Baby Sav-More.

http://orpheus.ucsd.edu/women/girls.htm
Girls and Parenting
Magazines Hip Mama Pregnancy Sabrina's Pregnancy Page Parenting Babyweb ChildLink San Diego: Parenting Resource Guide. (A complete guide to children and youth resources in the Greater San Diego area).

http://www.overlake.org/WebPage/ParentResources/parenting.htm
The goal of this section is to help Overlake parents find helpful information, articles, and books on topics related to parenting adolescents.

http://www.scescape.net/probe/magazines_family.html
Magazines for Families; Improve Homes and Family Relationships. Pull Down Menu for Magazines GQ Men's Fitness Men's Journal New Man Prime Health & Fitness. Pull Down Menu for Magazines American Legacy Ebony Essence Heart; Soul Jet Latina.

Parenting Books and Reference Materials

http://www.parentingpress.com/index.html
Parenting Press: Skill-Building Books for Parents and Teachers Introducing the Web Special: Special savings for orders placed through our secure on-line order form. Current special: 30% off Bully on the Bus when you order First Day Blues.

http://www.northwest-ap.org/bookstore.htm
Northwest Attachment Parenting's Bookstore
Browse Northwest Attachment Parenting's selections on any of the topics below: Pregnancy and Birth Breast-feeding Parenting Health and Nutrition Attachment Disorders Children's Books Do you know of any other good attachment parenting related books?

http://www.parentsplace.com/readroom/childnew/index.html
Children's Literature Home Page:
Children's Literature is designed to enhance children's literacy by helping adults find the best children's books available. We pore through the more than 3,000 new children's books published each year to find the very best to review in our newsletter.

http://www.geocity.com/Avenues/Family_and_Kids/Parenting
Family & Kids:Parenting
Recommended books pertaining to children

http://www.motherstuff.com/html/bibliography-pbook.htm
The Paper Pages - Parenting - Motherstuff
MaryHelen Lewis She's put together a bibliography of children's books
with strong female role models! School Is Dead: Home schooling
Resource Guides and How-to Books on Home schooling Extensive.

http://www.lesbian.org/lesbian-moms/biblios.html
Here are bibliographies for books covering various topics. BOOKS
ON LESBIAN AND GAY PARENTING AND FAMILIES Book
Reviews Books on gay parenting from AdoptionQuest. Gay Families
From Red and Black. Parenting Issues For Lesbians And Gay Men
From Amazon Bookstore in Minneapolis, MN.

http://www.tapestrybooks.com
ADOPTION BOOK CATALOG

http://www.activetraining.com
The home page of Active Training and Mel Silberman, trainer and
consultant, author of books on training and development, education
and parenting.

http://www.overlake.org
The goal of this section is to help Overlake parents find helpful
information, articles, and books on topics related to parenting
adolescents.

> *A disability is an ability to show the*
> *supremacy of the human spirit*
> *- Robert O. Owolabi*

Useful Internet Links
for Parents with Disabilities

Parents with Disabilities History and Mission

The Parents with Disabilities Program began in 1996 with a grant from the Pennsylvania Developmental Disabilities Council Managed by Project STAR, a program of The Children's Institute, this initiative is guided by an advisory council of parents with disabilities and professionals who share common beliefs and goals related to the rights of parents with disabilities to equal access in their communities.

The program ensures that parents with disabilities have the same opportunities as parents without disabilities to raise their children in home, family and community environments that are safe, secure, permanent and non-institutional.

http://www.curbcut.com/Parent.html
Links page for parents with disabilities. Includes bulletin board for sharing ideas with other disabled parents.

http://ourworld.compuserve.com/homepages/Trish_and_John/resource.htm
John's Resources: Parents with disabilities
Adaptive parenting equipment, medical and disability resources other parenting

http://www.lookingglass.org
Through The Looking Glass:
Berkeley, CA based community non-profit organization providing resources to families with a parent or child with disability.

http://www.ed.gov/offices/OSERS/NIDRR
National Institute on Disability and Rehabilitation Research Programs, research, grants and public policy issues relating to the disabled

http://www.netins.net/showcase/atforum
Assistive Technology-Disabled Sources and links to assistive technology for disabled.

http://www.infinitec.org
Infinitec Inc Assistive Technology resources

http://www.npnd.org
National Parent Network on Disabilities
The National Network on Disabilities is a nonprofit organization which was established to provide a national voice for parents of children, youth, and adults with special needs.

http://www.disabilitynet.co.uk
Disability Net is a worldwide information and news service for all disabled people and people with an interest in disability issues.

http://rainforest.parentsplace.com/dialog/get/disability.html
Parents with Disabilities; chat bulletin board; Interactive bulletin Parents with disabilities postings. Regional Contact for Parents with Disabilities 1-800-683-5898 for information on support groups, library services, assistive technology resources, area physicians and other health related services accessible to parents with disabilities.

The Family Resource Center

The Family Resource Center - Meeting children's special needs through parents

Mission
Helping children with special needs receive the love, hope, respect and services they need to achieve their full potential by strengthening their families and the professionals who serve them.

http://www.php.com/pti.htm
Parents Helping Parents is a parent-directed family resource center serving children with special needs, their families, and the professionals who serve them. Children with special needs are simply children that have a need for special services due to illness, accident, conditions of birth, learning differences or family stress. Founded in 1976, PHP is one of the oldest and largest children's charities of its kind in the United States. PHP is the family resource center for Early Start services in Santa Clara County, a Parent Training and Information Center for Northern California, and Information; Referral Center on a assistive technology for those with disabilities, the National Center for Parent-Directed Family Resource Centers in the United States, and a consultation and assistance agency for others starting or operating a PDFRC in the world.

Community Resources for Parents

http://www.parentsoup.com
ParentSoup

http://www.parentsplace.com/readroom/index.html
The Parenting Community: ParentsPlace.com: Reading Rooms operating under the belief that parents are the best resource for other parents in the adventure of child-rearing While the categories of the rooms below may not change often, the contents of the rooms are updated all the time.

http://www.parentsplace.com/readroom/index.html
The National Parenting Center
Founded in July of 1989, The National Parenting Center (TNPC) has become one of America's foremost parenting information services. Dedicated to providing parents with comprehensive and responsible guidance from nine of the world's most renowned child-rearing authorities, The National Parenting Center invites parents to expand their parenting skills and strengths.

http://www.positiveparenting.com
POSITIVE PARENTING (ON-LINE!)
Welcome to Positive Parenting, dedicated to providing resources and information to make parenting rewarding, effective and fun! We have classes and workshops in Ventura County . For parenting classes in your state, please visit our expert index.

http://www.parenthoodweb.com
ParenthoodWeb -- Parenting, Pregnancy, Family, Child care, Breast-feeding and Infant Health resources. The award-winning online parenting, pregnancy and family community for parents and prospective parents. Free expert advice, discussion groups chat, polls, recall information and birth announcements. Featured in Newsweek & Redbook.

http://www.kcts.org/product/single/tip12.htm
Family Help Line for supportive listening, crisis intervention, free parenting handouts, and statewide information and referrals to parents. In Seattle, call 233-0139; elsewhere in Washington State, call 1-800-932-HOPE.

http://stmichael.stillwater.mn.us/learn/resource/r01.html
Family, Marriage, and Parenting - St. Michael's Parish Resource Center Updated December 12, 1997 Category # Case Against Divorce, The Medved, Diane Choosing to Love Ford, Edward E

Christian Families in the Real World Finley, Mitch & Kathy.

http://www.geocity.com/Avenues/Family_and_Kids/Parenting
GeoCities - Family & Kids: Visit home pages on Parenting listed below. Don't forget to vote for the best! Enchanted Forest, pop. 49,362 Heartland pop. 141,933 Mommies and Daddies, Newborns, toddlers, adolescents and teenagers.

http://www.pampers.com
Pampers Parenting Institute
Pampers Parenting Institute - In-depth information on child-care: Helping your baby sleep through the night; Encouraging healthy development; Caring for your baby when sick; Keeping your baby's delicate skin healthy; Also Product information is also available.

http://www.onnow.com/excite/listing/TextChat50.shtml
Subject: Text Chat Date / Time Parent Issues. Issues parents face in educating their children. Every Tue 7:00 PM ParentChat with D! Join this Question &&Answer hour with CPO Host ~ Deborah. With experience in many areas of parenting you will be sure to find your answer here!

Doing nothing gets pretty tiresome because you can't stop and rest.   - Unknown

> *Put not your trust in money, but put your money in trust. - Oliver Wendell Holmes*

> *Keep your face to the sunshine and you cannot see the shadow. - Helen Keller*

> *It is easier to forgive an enemy than a friend.*
> *- Dorothee Deluzy*

Order Form

✳ Fax orders: (301) 990-2393

☎ Telephone orders: Call (301) 977-3442. Have your
   AMEX, Optima, Discover, VISA or MasterCard ready.

☐ E-mail orders: bobowo@aol.com
   On-line orders: http://members.aol.com/bobowo

✉ Postal Orders: Bob & Bob Associates, Inc., P.O. Box
   10246, Gaithersburg, MD 20898-0246

**Please send the following book: "Effective Parenting" by Robert
O. Owolabi   ($4.95)**
I understand that I may return the book for a full refund - for any
reason, no questions asked.

Company Name:_____

Name:_____

Address:_____

City:_____State:_____Zip:_____-_____

Telephone: (____) _____

Shipping:
$1.50 for the first book and $0.75 for each additional book.

Payment:
❏ Check   ❏ Money Order (*Made payable to: Bob & Bob
Associates, Inc.*)   ❏ Credit Card: ❏ VISA, ❏ MasterCard,
❏ Optima, ❏ AMEX, ❏ Discover
Card number:_____
Name on card:_____Exp. Date:_____/____

As a parent, remember to always repeat everything you say, at least, five times.
- Unknown

Dressing small children is not as easy as it seems: First, buy an octopus and a string bag. Attempt to put the octopus into the string bag so that none of the arms hangs out. Time allowed for this: all morning!!!
- Unknown

It takes a person who is wide awake to make his dream come true.   - Roger Babson

Order Form

✳   Fax orders: (301) 990-2393

☎   Telephone orders: Call (301) 977-3442. Have your
     AMEX, Optima, Discover, VISA or MasterCard ready.

□   E-mail orders: bobowo@aol.com
     On-line orders: http://members.aol.com/bobowo

✉   Postal Orders: Bob & Bob Associates, Inc., P.O. Box
     10246, Gaithersburg, MD 20898-0246

**Please send the following book: "Effective Parenting" by Robert
O. Owolabi   ($4.95)**
I understand that I may return the book for a full refund - for any
reason, no questions asked.

Company Name:_____

Name:_____

Address:_____

City:_____State:_____Zip:_____-_____

Telephone: (____) _____

Shipping:
$1.50 for the first book and $0.75 for each additional book.
Payment:
❑   Check ❑   Money Order (*Made payable to: Bob & Bob
Associates, Inc.*)   ❑ Credit Card: ❑ VISA, ❑ MasterCard,
❑ Optima, ❑ AMEX, ❑ Discover
Card number:_____

Name on card:_____Exp. Date:_____/____

> *It's not the quantity but the quality of reading that stimulates thought.*
> *- Validivar*

> *The glory of a deed is in finishing it to the very end.   - Jengis Khan*